PORTRAITS IN POWER

David Cameron, Boris Johnson and Alan Johnson

Nigel Cawthorne

Table of Contents

David Cameron: Class Act

Blond Ambition: The Rise and Rise of Boris Johnson

Alan Johnson: Left Standing

David Cameron

Class Act

Chapter One – Distinguished Forebears

David Cameron is all things to all people. This is not a jibe. Launching a campaign on Britishness in 2007, he said: "My father's side of the family, by being Camerons, are predominantly Scottish. On my mother's side of the family, her mother was a Llewellyn, so Welsh. I'm a real mixture of Scottish, Welsh, and English. Her grandmother's side were Scottish Empire builders – conquered all sorts of parts of India, I think." Not only that, when Cameron visited Israel in 2014, he told the Knesset that his great-great-grandfather was Jewish. This lead Dr Yaakov Wise, a research fellow at the University of Manchester Centre for Jewish Studies, to aver that he was possibly a direct descendent of Moses.

David Cameron's great-great-grandfather Ewen Cameron left the family seat near Culloden in Inverness-shire early in the reign of Queen Victoria. After a few years with the Caledonian Bank, he joined the Bank of Hindustan, China and Japan, who sent him to their Hong Kong branch. Then when the Bank of Hindustan went into liquidation, he joined the newly formed Hong Kong and Shanghai Banking Corporation, now known as HSBC, rising to become the head of its London office. He was knighted in 1901 for his services to banking and went on to play a key role arranging loans from the Rothschild family for Japan during the Russo-Japanese War of 1904-5.

His son Ewen Allan Cameron became a senior partner in the international stockbrokers and investment bank Panmure Gordon & Co. He married Rachel Geddes, whose father, Chicago's grain king Alexander Geddes, returned to his native Scotland in the 1880s and built the mansion Blairmore House in the foothills of the Grampians.

Their son Donald also became a partner in Panmure Gordon. It was through the company that his met his future wife Enid Agnes Maud Levita. This is where the Jewish connection comes in. Her grandfather was Emile Levita, who arrived in Britain from Germany in the 1850s. In 1871, he was granted British citizenship and became a director of the Charter Bank of India, Australia and China, which became Standard Chartered Bank in 1969.

Dr Wise has traced the family's ancestral line back to Elijah Levita (1469-1549), a central figure in the "Christian Hebraist" movement, who pioneered Hebrew and Yiddish linguistic research at the time of the Tudors.

The name Levita is the Latin form of Levite, meaning a Jew descended from the tribe of Levi, the son of Jacob, and one of the original twelve tribes of Israel. According to Dr Wise, the leader of the Levites at the time of the exodus from Egypt was Moses. Modern-day Levites often carry the surname Levy, Levitan or Levita.

Having naturalized, Emile Levita adopted all the trappings of an English gentleman, owning a grouse moor in Wales and sending his four sons to Eton. One son, Cecil, became the chairman of the London County Council in 1928, while Arthur became a stockbroker with Panmure Gordon. He married Stephanie Cooper, the granddaughter of Lady Elizabeth FitzClarence, who in turn was the daughter of William IV and his mistress, the actress Dorothea Jordan. This makes David Cameron the fifth cousin of the Queen, once removed.

Steffie Cooper was well connected. Her father was royal surgeon Sir Alfred Cooper, an expert in venereal disease, while her mother was known in society for her two elopements and a divorce. Between them, Sir Alfred boasted, they had inspected the private parts of half the peers in London. Steffie's uncle was the Duke of Fife. Her aunt, his wife, was Louise, Princess Royal, eldest daughter of Edward VII. And her brother was Duff Cooper, a prominent and raffish Conservative MP who became Minister of Information in Winston Churchill's wartime cabinet. Through him, David Cameron is related to the publisher Rupert Hart-Davis, the historian John Julius Norwich, TV presenter Adam Hart-Davis, and journalist and writer Duff Hart-Davis.

There was another politician on that side of the family, General Sir James Duff, an army officer and MP for Banffshire in Scotland during the late 1700s. He was awarded £4,101, equivalent to more than £3million today, to compensate him for the 202 slaves he forfeited on the Grange Sugar Estate in Jamaica when slavery was abolished in the British colonies in 1833.

It was at Blairmore House that their daughter, Enid Cameron, née Levita, gave birth to David Cameron's father, Ian, who was born with both legs severely deformed. He underwent a series of operations in an attempt to correct them, but they remained foreshortened in comparison to the rest of his body. While special provision had to be made for him at his prep school, his mother pushed him to overcome his disabilities.

By the time Ian was ready to go to Eton, his father had left his mother and married an aristocratic Austrian divorcee who had been a family friend. They set up home in Kensington, while Ian remained with his mother in Knightsbridge. She married a younger son of Baron Manton, whose family included Baron Hesketh, the Conservative chief whip in the House of Lords from 1991 to 1993.

Despite his disability, Ian Cameron was an enthusiastic sportsman at Eton, ruing only that he could not ski. He was strong, outgoing and courageous.

Instead of going on to university, Ian trained as an accountant. He did not enjoy it and forbade his children to follow in his footsteps. Working hard he eventually followed his father and grandfather to become a partner in Panmure Gordon, though he admitted he got the position partly due to nepotism.

He moved out of his mother's house and found a flat around the corner in Basil Street, where he threw endless parties. He loved to dance and attracted society beauties.

When Donald Cameron died, he left his son over £57,000, the equivalent of £1million today. Ian then married twenty-seven-year-old former debutante Mary Mount who, if anything, came from an even more distinguished background which included a long line of Tory politicians. This began with Sir William Mount of Wasing

Place, Berkshire, who was MP for Yarmouth from 1818 to 1819, then for Newport on the Isle of Wight from 1831 to 1832, before he became High Sheriff of Berkshire. His son Sir William George Mount was MP for Newbury, High Sheriff and Chairman of the Berkshire County Council. His son was Sir William Mount, 1st Baronet, and was also MP for Newbury and Chairman of Berkshire County Council. His son was Sir William Malcolm Mount, 2nd Baronet, and again became High Sheriff of Berkshire, still maintaining the family estate at Wasing Place. The 3rd Baronet was Sir William Robert Ferdinand Mount, who styles himself simply as Ferdinand Mount, a columnist for the *Sunday Times* and head of Mrs Thatcher's policy unit in 10 Downing Street, 1983-83. They had all been to Eton and Oxford.

The Mounts' entry in *Burke's Peerage* carries the name of David Cameron at the bottom and there is a cross reference to the Talbot family, which comes under the entry for the Earl of Shrewsbury and Waterford. The 22nd Earl of Shrewsbury is now the Premier Earl of England. The original title was created in 1442 for John Talbot, the heroic general who lost his life at Castillon in the final battle of the Hundred Years War. Two of his sons were killed with him, one legitimate, the other a bastard. The French honoured his courage, calling him "the English Achilles".

"In terms of English history, the Talbots are one of the great families, like the Cecils or the Churchills, only much older," said William Rees-Mogg, formerly the long-serving editor of *The Times*.

Among the family, they number bishops, archbishops, Lord Chancellors and a Prime Minister – though before the term was coined. Charles Talbot, the 12th Earl and first and only Duke of Shrewsbury – as well as being Charles II's godson – became First Minister to William III, Queen Anne and George I. It has to be said, the Talbots, the Mounts and, latterly, the Camerons are top draw.

The 2nd Baronet, Sir William Malcolm Mount, married Elizabeth Nance Llewellyn, who's second daughter, Mary Fleur Mount, married Ian Cameron. The marriage was conventional and successful. Their son David William Donald Cameron was born in London on 9 October 1966 and christened at the Mount family chapel in Wasing Place. He has an older brother, Alexander Allan, born in 1963, who went on to become a barrister and QC; and two sisters – Tania Rachel, born in 1965, and Clare Louise, born in 1971.

In 1986, the family benefited from another windfall. In the "Big Bang" – the financial deregulation of the City of London – Panmure Gordon was sold for a fortune. In 2007, it was estimated that Ian Cameron was worth at least £10million.

Chapter Two – Eton Rifles

When David Cameron was around three, the family moved from Phillimore Place in Kensington to the village of Peasemore in Berkshire. His father Ian commuted from the station at Didcot Parkway to the City of London, where he had also become a director of the estate agents John D. Wood. He was chairman of White's, the gentlemen's club in St James's, and had a passion for racehorses, owning a number of them, including one he thought might win the Derby. In 1977, he took his eleven-year-old son David to see Red Rum win the Grand National at Aintree.

David's mother Mary sat as a magistrate in Newbury and the children were brought up by Gwen Hoare, who had been in service to the Mount family for her entire adult life. She had been Mary's nanny at Wasing, then moved to Phillimore Place to look after Alexander.

The family lived in the Old Rectory. Ian Cameron was a church warden and Mary was on the flower-arranging rota. Dinner was served promptly at 7.45 pm. Impeccable manners were required. Afterwards there would be parlour games. On more formal occasions, the women-folk would withdraw while, from a young age, David would hold forth.

They had a tennis court and a swimming pool, which were open to friends. Children from the village resented not being invited. While the atmosphere at home was often bookish; outdoors the children enjoyed country pursuits. There were chickens to feed, dogs to walk and pigeons, rabbits and rooks to shoot. Later their father would take the boys shooting on Woolley Park, the country estate of the Wroughtons, another great Conservative family who provided Berkshire with High Sheriffs.

But it was tennis that was David's great passion, though he was equally competitive as a bowler and a batsman, especially at the annual cricket match held between teams raised by him and his brother, which was played at either Peasemore or Wasing.

David and Alexander shared a room until they went to prep school at the age of seven. Though they teased each other, they were eager to please. Their parents rarely had to raise their voice to them. School reports were read out formally by their father before the boys had a chance to see them. If they had fallen below standards, his father would merely say, in reproof: "I see."

Once, when David had got into a scrape at Eton, his father simply told him that he did not pay the massive school fees for him to break the rules.

Neighbour and school friend Pete Czernin said: "His parents were fantastic. They were never pushy with their children; they gave them all implicit confidence without cockiness."

"Dave inherited his father's cheek and energy and his mother's common sense – he's very uncomplicated," said cousin Ferdinand Mount. "He was the kind of boy who did his homework and then had a good time with his friends.''

Cameron particularly looked up to his father.

"I never thought of my father as disabled. He was always so optimistic," he said. "He is my role model. Dad has never let his disability hold him back. He has proved that you can do anything you want in life. He was an amazingly brave man. I think I got my sense of optimism from him."

And he was uncomplaining.

"Whingeing wasn't on the menu," one family member told the *Guardian* and a friend talked of the "subconscious drive that Dave has got from Ian's incredible example. Ian has vast enthusiasm – which Dave inherited and a sort of unstoppableness."

Cameron particularly remembered his father's diligence.

"My father used to work really long days but he always had time for the parochial church council and the parish council," he said.

Before the 2010 election, he also thanked his mum and dad for their values.

At the age of seven, David Cameron followed older brother Alex to Heatherdown Preparatory School at Winkfield, near Ascot. The school boasted among its alumni Prince Andrew and Prince Edward. The Queen would sometimes appear in a green station-wagon to drop off her sons. Once she turned up at the school play to see the young David Cameron dressed as a rabbit.

For the first term, the new boys were kept in an annex called Heatherlea, where they were cosseted and allowed pillow fights. Once they were accustomed to being away from home, they were put on a stricter regime, sleeping in a dormitory of twelve where the only comforts allowed were their own teddy and a rug brought from home to cover the wooden floorboards.

Religion framed the day. There were prayers before breakfast and service in the chapel before supper. All the masters came from public schools and the teaching methods were old fashioned. The books of the Bible, Latin declensions, and the dates of the kings and queens of England were learnt by rote.

A tubby child, Cameron said he "lost a stone every term because the helpings were so small". Otherwise, a teacher said he was "a natural boarding-school boy … easy to get on with … just a middle-class boy from a nice family".

Heatherdown was also unrepentantly posh. At sports day, there were three loos – Ladies, Gentlemen and Chauffeurs.

"It was deadly serious," said former teacher Rhidian Llewellyn. "The drivers were not supposed to mix with the other guests."

One can only supposed that the pilots of the two or three helicopters that flew some of the parents in were also allowed to use the Chauffeurs' loo.

Along with the Queen, the parents of the "toffs", as Llewellyn called them, included two Princesses, two Marchionesses, one Viscount, one Earl, one Lord, four Sirs, eight Honourables, one Commodore, one Brigadier, one Major and two Captains. One pupil, the son of an MP, said with slight exaggeration that he was one of the few boys who did not change their name during their time there due to some inherited title.

One of the virtues inculcated into the boys was *noblesse oblige.* Another was good manners. When he felt that the standards were slipping, the headmaster sent the boys out on the rugby pitch to doff their caps to the corner flags. Otherwise discipline was administered with a clothes brush to the seat of the trousers. David Cameron suffered this punishment after stealing strawberries from the kitchen garden.

Among Cameron's closest friends was Peter Getty, grandson of the oil tycoon John Paul Getty. In 1978, to celebrate Getty's twelfth birthday, Cameron and three other boys, with Llewellyn as chaperone, flew on Concorde to Washington DC, courtesy of Getty, with the eleven-year-old David swigging free glasses of Dom Pérignon '69. After driving around DC in an air-conditioned Lincoln Convertible, they went sight-seeing in New York, before flying on to Disney World and the Kennedy Space Centre in Florida, Las Vegas, the Grand Canyon, Hollywood and Getty's home in Pacific Heights in San Francisco.

That year, according to his school report, Cameron was ranked last in the sixth form, following poor results in Latin, maths, geography and French. However, his former headmaster James Edwards leapt to his defence, saying he was no "dunce", rather the opposite, as he had been promoted into the sixth form at the age of eleven. Dissenting, Llewellyn said that Edwards picked "the stable rather than the colt". If a boy came from the right background, he was selected. Heatherdown's job was to prepare boys for Eton. In the summer of 1979, Cameron passed his Common Entrance exam and was accepted.

At Eton, Cameron at last had a room of his own and got used to wearing a tailcoat. He also had the protection of his older brother, who was a popular boy three years above him. But this meant he also had to live in his shadow. While Alex excelled academically, Cameron minor's performance was considered mediocre. He was not at the bottom of the class, nor was he at the top. His maths teacher did not even remember him, though he recalled all the other boys who went on to be famous.

The same lapse afflicted David Guilford, who remembered teaching Classics to Boris Johnson. Guilford said: "I also taught David Cameron, but I don't remember him at all – he must just have done what he was told."

Others remember that Cameron could hold his own and showed an interest in literature, music and art – thought not politics. He had no grounding in it.

"Although I'm sure my parents voted Conservative," he said, "it wasn't an especially political household."

He was kind to other boys and made friends at school that he would keep for the rest of his life. But outside school, he was said to be "a typical Etonian, rather full of himself". A contemporary, Marcus Warren, said: "Cameron was posh, even by the standards of Eton."

Although Cameron said he "wasn't a complete rebel", he did enjoy a sly cigarette and a swig of wine or beer behind the cricket pavilion.

At thirteen, journalist Caroline Graham says he was an "expert kisser". He admitted to having a poster of the American model Cheryl Tiegs in a pink bikini and, sheepishly, the bare-bottomed Athena tennis girl on his wall. Otherwise his interests were art and sport.

He claimed that The Jam's "Eton Rifles" was one of his favourite songs and he was in the cadet corps, the target of the track. He also learnt the drum break from Phil Collins' "In the Air Tonight", which is also thought to be a favourite of Ed Miliband. Cameron used a UB40 track as the accompaniment to a presentation he did on poverty and unemployment. He then announced that he wished to be called "Dave". It was cooler.

At sixteen, he already had a girlfriend, Lydia Craig, now Lydia Dickinson, the daughter of a fine-art auctioneer who was a good friend of his father. The couple had joined blonde Lucy Wigram – now Lucy Sangster – the daughter of property developer Anthony Wigram and her date at the 1983 Freedom Ball at the Café Royal near Piccadilly. They danced to the outrageous ska band Bad Manners and raised £7,000 for Amnesty International. Lydia went on to be a designer on *Penthouse* magazine.

She was the first of many. "Dave never had any trouble pulling," said one of his friends. He liked aristocratic girls with an artistic side to them and went out with "some real crackers".

Six weeks before taking his O-Levels, Cameron was caught smoking cannabis. He admitted the offence and had not been involved in selling drugs, so he was not expelled, but was fined,

15

confined to school grounds, barred from Open Day and given a "Georgic". This was a punishment that involved copying out five hundred lines of Latin text. He took his punishment manfully and did not split on the others involved.

He has described his twelve O-levels as "not very good", but he got three As at A-level, in history, history of art and economics with politics. It was only then that he "got going academically," he said. One teacher described him as a late developer.

In history, he specialized in the Spanish Civil War. His topic in art history was Augustus Pugin, but not for his work on the Palace of Westminster, but that at Chirk Castle in Wales, as he had private access through a relative. In 1983 he won the Trials Prize for Politics, then went on to study the Troubles in Northern Ireland. But his biggest mention in the Eton school magazine was when he sprained his ankle dancing to bagpipes on a school trip to Rome. He explained that they were busking on the Spanish Steps to raise money for booze.

Outside his schoolwork, Cameron did not get involved in politics at Eton, even during the furore that gripped the school when the school magazine published an article by James Wood attacking Thatcherism. But the seeds had been sown. John Clarke, who taught Cameron politics as he prepared for Oxford, said: "I'm pretty sure I viewed him as politically ambitious even then. He was articulate and politically motivated and interested. He was interested in the business of politics, in politics as a profession, even at that stage. I don't think he'd planned it out in the way Heseltine is supposed to have done. He found politics stimulating, in a good pragmatic Conservative way."

Friends said he already had ambitions to be Prime Minister. But Cameron denied making Michael Heseltine-like career plans that would take him step by step to the top office.

"Even at university I didn't know what I was going to do next," he said.

Besides, becoming Prime Minister then seemed out of the question in the meritocratic eighties. One of his friends at Eton remembered walking with Cameron between lessons and looking up at the statues of past Etonian Prime Ministers.

"We were convinced there would never be an Etonian Prime Minister again," he said. "I certainly didn't think Dave would have a go at it. His only acting roles at school were as a serving-man and as a girl. He was never outrageously extrovert – just quietly popular."

Still, there were stirrings. He bristled against the "Common Market" and wrote a thoughtful review of a talk by former Labour industry minister Eric Heffer. In his formative years, he took his inspiration from far and wide.

"One of the books that got me interested in politics was Tony Benn's *Arguments for Democracy*, which is just a great book," he said. "Lots of it I disagree with, but I loved reading it. I like being stimulated by things I disagree with, almost rather than reading something and saying: 'Yes, that is my creed.'"

Though he attended Eton's Political Society – whose guest speakers during his time included Lord Home, Lord Carrington,

Frank Field, William Waldegrave, Grey Gowrie and Len Murray – he was not on the committee like Boris Johnson, so he did not get a chance to talk with the speakers or dine with them afterwards. But then he had connections of his own, and went to Downing Street to interview Ferdinand Mount for the school magazine.

School chums talked of his assuredness – which some would dismiss as arrogance. Others said that he embodied the Etonian sense of entitlement, in contrast to other alumni who felt uneasy at the idea of privilege. He was not, however, a member of Pop – Eton's self-elected elite. He did become captain of his house though.

With politics now his forte, his tutors advised studying philosophy, politics and economics at Brasenose College, Oxford. He sat the entrance exam at the end of the Michaelmas Term, after sitting his A levels the term before. This so-called "seventh term" entrance has since been banned as it gave too much of an advantage to the public schools. At his interview, he was caught out bluffing about how much philosophy he had read, but was accepted anyway.

Before going up to Oxford to study Philosophy, Politics and Economics he took a gap year, working initially for his godfather, Sussex MP Tim Rathbone, who he described as "a nice guy but a bit of a wet". Rathbone was expelled from the Conservative Party for supporting the pro-European Conservatives in the 1999 Euro-elections. As an intern, Cameron would watch debates in the House of Commons from the public gallery and witnessed Enoch Powell in action.

After three months, Cameron went to work as a shipping agent for Jardine Matheson in Hong Kong, a job he had secured through a friend of his father. Company accommodation was provided and he got a taste of expatriate life. Three months later, he moved on to Japan, then headed homewards on the Trans-Siberian Railway.

While taking a short break at a Black Sea resort on the way, he claimed that an attempt was made to recruit him and a school friend as KGB agents. It would be interesting to think of David Cameron as the Kim Philby *de nos jours*.

Chapter Three – Buller Boy

David Cameron went up to Oxford in 1985 to read PPE at Brasenose College, which had resisted pressure to take in more students from state schools. Though he worked hard, he also relished his spare time. With his sister, he took Mick Jagger's daughter Jade punting. The next day Jagger phoned Cameron's mother demanding: "What's all this my daughter has been getting up to with your son?"

Apparently Mick had misheard the word "punting" and mistaken it for "hunting" – despite having sympathy for the devil, he disapproved of blood sports.

Cameron also hung out at Hi-Lo café with its Rastafarian owner Hugh "Andy" Anderson.

"David was very interested in his music," said the Jamaican, who had come to the UK in the 1960s. "We talked about reggae, blues, jazz all sorts of things. He was one of our regulars in the mid to late eighties and, like a lot of people, I think he kept coming back because he liked the atmosphere."

When Andy had to serve a drink to a customer, he would hand his one-year-old son to David, who would bounce the child on his knee in front of the television. Like many a student addict of daytime television, he never missed *Going for Gold* with Henry Kelly.

"David never mentioned anything about his interest in politics," said Andy. "I only found out about his interest from one of his friends."

According to fellow student Steve Rathbone, Cameron avoided student politics because "he wanted to have a good time". Amidst the political turmoil of the time, there was no doubt that he was a rabid Thatcherite though.

Nevertheless Rathbone – a state-educated "Stain", in Eton parlance – said: "He was clearly an Etonian, but he wasn't swaggering around in a braying, Sloaney way. Equally, he wasn't trying to be something he wasn't. He never tried to adopt an estuary accent, as many students do from major public schools, or wear right-on trendy clothes. He was a good mate of people from very different backgrounds."

Polite and hardworking, it was clear that Cameron was out to get a First, spouting Locke and Hume confidently in seminars. However, he did not take the easy option of dropping one of his subjects and taking an extra paper in the other two.

"He partied too," said James Fergusson, a chum from school, "but he was incredibly organized about it."

That included donning a tailcoat for smart dinner parties, though he won plaudits from other quarters when he persuaded Dr Feelgood to play at the college's May Ball. And, of course, he was a member of the Bullingdon Club.

Thought to have been founded in 1780 as an all-male sporting club, its membership was limited to thirty, by invitation only. Over the years it had become a dining and drinking club. Members dressed for their annual Club dinner in hand-tailored navy blue tailcoats with a velvet collar, offset with ivory silk lapels, brass monogrammed buttons, a mustard waistcoat, and a sky blue bow tie. Only old Etonians need apply. David Cameron, George Osborne and Boris Johnson were all members. Bullers drunken antics were legendary. During the Thatcher years, it was said, they were at their snobbish and self-regarding worst.

"If you weren't socially interesting, one of the in-crowd, he would be very dismissive," a contemporary said.

Part of the initiation was to have your room ransacked. When Cameron returned to find the place trashed, he reported it to the Dean, who then wanted to know the names of the culprits. The Bullers had a code of silence, so he had to bear the penalty alone.

Though it was natural for Cameron to join such an elite institution, he avoided its excesses. No one ever saw him uncontrollably drunk.

"Dave is a cautious man," said another friend, "someone who would think twice before throwing a bottle at a policeman."

The joke was that Cameron went along to Bullingdon dinners for the conversation – "a bit like the man who buys *Playboy* magazine for the interviews," said Cameron's biographers Francis Elliott and James Hanning. On the famous night when a plant pot was thrown through a restaurant window, the police were called and Boris Johnson put on a surprising turn of speed. Cameron retired early and was at home tucked up in bed.

Cameron was also a member of another dining club called the Octagon. Their uniform was a brown tailcoat with yellow lapels and a yellow bow-tie.

According to the club's records, on 19 February 1987, members "met for dinner in Mr Cameron's rooms in celebration of the St Valentine's day's massacre". Alongside a list of female guests was written "You sexy things" and "There have never been sexier waitresses; methinks my mind doth split at the thought".

Close to Mr Cameron's signature was the name Fran Ferguson, who was his long-term university girlfriend – though in his first term, he dated Catherine Snow, niece of banker Charles Hambro and stepdaughter of Viscount Hampden. Another flame was Alice Rayman, who went on to marry the son of former Tory Cabinet Minister Lord King.

Another night, an Octagon dinner was held at the Luna Caprese, an Italian restaurant in north Oxford.

"Preprandial drinks were taken in Mr Cameron's rooms", the record said, then the members embarked on a seven-course meal, including turtle and sherry soup. There was a five-course wine list, beginning with Corvo Duca di Salaparuta, passing through Marguerite Christel Champagne and ending with the club's stable tipple, Graham's 1977 port.

In a rare political act, he had a party in his room in June 1987 to celebrate Margaret Thatcher's third election victory. Otherwise, he left the politics of the Oxford Union and the University Conservative Association to the likes of Boris Johnson, Michael Gove and the other rising stars of the Tory Party. He only attended the Union if there was an interesting speaker. He supported the decision to let Gerry Adams speak there, though regretted it afterwards.

After eighteen months, Cameron bowed out of the Octagon. He took a temporary job shifting crates to earn enough money to take a holiday with Fran at her parent's place in Kenya. To impress her parents he brought a gift with him. It was a Monty Python record that included a sketch joking about Hitler. Fran's mother was German. Nevertheless she was sufficiently impressed to tell Fran "that chap is going to be Prime Minister one day".

As for Cameron, he had such a good time he missed his plane home and had to stay another week.

Though they enjoyed each other's company, David and Fran split up after eighteen months as she took up too much of this time when he wanted to study.

"I wanted to have arguments and be distracted, but when someone is very ambitious and wants to get a First, they don't want someone demanding too much of them," she said. "I was also quite jealous and would provoke him to try to shake him out of his self-assuredness."

Fran was so upset when the affair ended she tried to get a friend to intercede for her. Cameron was unbending, though he still wanted her to like him.

Others girls were picked up at sherry parties or in the Playpen nightclub. Women, it seemed, were attracted to his sweet nature – he cried openly at the end of a play or film.

Seizing another chance to travel, he renewed his acquaintanceship with America on a five-week sojourn at California's Stanford University, where he wowed fellow students with his unwitting impersonation of Hugh Grant.

After two years living in college, Cameron moved into private accommodation with some friends. Sometimes he would cook – pheasant was his signature dish. Otherwise there was a kebab shop close by, or the Hi-Lo where he would eat jerk chicken and goat curry, washed down with Red Stripe or overproof rum. There was plenty of booze back at the house too.

One of his housemates, Giles Andreae, who was also a family friend, was diagnosed with cancer and underwent a debilitating course of chemotherapy. Cameron drove him down to Peasemore in his battered Volvo and tended him there. He even took time off during his finals to look in on his friend.

While Cameron shied away from university politics, he could not avoid the current debates which were plainly part of his course. One of his tutors was Vernon Bogdanor, an informal advisor to the Social and Liberal Democrats, which morphed into the Liberal Democrats in 1989. This did nothing to shake Cameron's position as a pragmatic centrist Conservative. As a result, he lost little sleep over the broader philosophical questions he confronted in his philosophy course. Nevertheless, he put in the work to get a First. He conceded later that it was naff to be proud of your degree, but he was proud.

Chapter Four – The World of Westminster

It may seem odd that a man who showed little interest in frontline politics at university should storm Westminster as soon as he left. In fact, David Cameron had applied for a number of jobs in the City and journalism before his finals, and been turned down. But some "judicious prodding" from Buckingham Palace landed him a job at Conservative Central Office.

Robin Harris, the director of the research department there, said: "He applied to the research department, but there were no spaces. Then we received a call from a royal equerry wanting to know why he had not been hired."

When the story came out, Cameron admitted that strings were pulled on his behalf by some at the Palace.

"I had a godmother whose husband worked there, who knew Robin or something," he said. "Anyway, I hope he doesn't regret employing me."

Cameron's godmother was Fiona Aird, whose husband Captain Sir Alastair Aird was variously comptroller and equerry to the Queen Mother. Others have suggested that the puppet master was neighbour and family friend Sir Brian McGath, private secretary to Prince Philip, though he was a referee for the job. Both denied making the call. Nevertheless, it can't hurt to have friends in high places, though other candidates were understandably disgruntled.

He started work in Smith Square in September 1988. The Conservative research department is the fast-track to high political office, as other alumni will attest. Then it was full of right-wing zealots who called Mrs Thatcher "mother". Cameron was handed the Trade and Industry, Energy and Privatization portfolio. He worked hard, shone and his natural sociability won him friends, many of whom proved useful when his political career took off. Among them were fellow Old Etonian Ed Llewellyn who became his Downing Street Chief of Staff and Ed Vaizey, son of Lord Vaizey and a something of a star at Oxford, who became Minister of Culture. Other inmates were equally well connected.

Catherine Fall became his Deputy Chief of Staff. Steve Hilton, who he used to take holidays with, became his director of strategy. And Peter Campbell became a special advisor who helped Cameron prepare for Prime Minister's Questions.

Outside the inner circle of high-fliers, Cameron's brisk manner was sometimes considered bumptious, if not bullying – a man who liked to make himself look good at the expense of others appearing stupid, it was said. Not for him boozy lunches or a glass of wine in the office. He worked long hours and was clearly fiercely ambitious. He was also known for his good manner and all the girls in Conservative HQ fancied him. In 1990, he started an office romance with Laura Adshead, daughter of a prominent diplomatic family. When he broke it off, she had to take compassionate leave to recover. Later, Laura had problems with alcohol and drugs. There was speculation that this was fall-out from the affair. Eventually she became a nun.

Another girlfriend who was upset when they parted was Lisa de Savary, daughter of property developer Peter de Savary. She fell for him in a big way, according to a friend, but "Dave kind of dumped her and she was very cross. It all left rather a nasty taste."

The break-up did not put Lisa off politics. She managed her father's campaign as a parliamentary candidate for James Goldsmith's Referendum Party, and later married a banker and went to live in Bahrain.

The research department again offered a chance to travel. Within a few months of starting, he took an all-expenses-paid trip to apartheid South Africa. The trip was laid on by lobbyists Strategy Network International, later embroiled in the cash-for-questions scandal. Civil servants were told to shun these lavish jollies but, to the members of the Conservative research department, they were considered a perk. Cameron's travelling companion on this trip was a gay, black, master of foxhounds Derek Laud, who went on to become a contestant on *Big Brother*.

The job was not terribly well paid and Cameron shared a flat in South Kensington with his old friend Pete Czernin, whose wealthy family could trace its roots back to Tudor times. Interviewed in 2005, Czernin, then a film producer, apologized that he had not dirt to dish.

"You're never going to get Dave in a 'Six-in-a-Bed Supermodel Drug Orgy'," he said. "Sorry, that's just not Dave."

Indeed, Cameron now refused a joint when offered it; his eyes were firmly set on a political career. He was more interested in debating over the dinner table. Friends said that it was there that he learnt all the tricks – playing to the gallery, puncturing a counter argument with a quip, changing the subject, overwhelming the enemy with facts and figures. He was always out to win the argument, whatever the cost.

The director of the research department's political section, Guy Black, spotted Cameron's killer instinct to spot and exploit an opponent's weakness and poached him. And when Black moved on, Cameron stepped in as his replacement.

Although she had won three elections, Mrs Thatcher was becoming increasingly unpopular over the poll tax. As head of the political section, Cameron attended a secret strategy meeting at Hever Castle in Kent. This put him in with Andrew Lansley, the new head of the research department.

Lansley had decided the department's strategy. Now they were act as if the Conservatives were in opposition, taking every opportunity to attack Labour leader Neil Kinnock to distract attention from the government's problems. In charge of this negative campaigning was David Cameron who was to brief Cabinet ministers on what line to take in media appearances.

When Nigel Lawson resigned as Chancellor, Cameron accurately spotted that Mrs Thatcher's days were numbered. Subtly, he swung behind Michael Heseltine, now seen as the coming man.

Nevertheless, when Mrs Thatcher finally resigned, he said he was "very sad", though he had only met her twice.

"The first should have ended my political career before it even began," he said when a new MP. "I was the trade researcher at Central Office and she asked me what the trade deficit was. I didn't know.

"The second was at her birthday lunch a couple of years ago. She commiserated that Labour had stolen Tory language, which she acknowledged made fighting them more difficult. Fixing me with her famous stare, she said there was one thing they would never understand – the importance of 'liberty under the rule of law'."

With John Major rather than Heseltine replacing Mrs Thatcher as PM, Cameron was eager to make a good impression. Over eager, perhaps. Attending a debate in the House of Commons, he inadvertently sat in a box reserved for civil servants, inviting a rebuke from the Speaker that earned him his first mention in the national newspapers.

Under the new regime, Cameron's first job was to write a guide to the campaign should Major decide to go to the country, working closely with Saatchi & Saatchi. He was then called into Downing Street to help Major prepare for PMQs, while new MP David Davis became, effectively, his goffer, running friendly questions to loyal backbenchers.

On 30 June 1991, the Atticus column on the *Sunday Times* mentioned that Cameron was responsible for Major's performance which had "become sharper of late". He had "Neil Kinnock squirming on Thursday when he brandished a dreadful piece of doublespeak from Tony Blair, Labour's employment spokesman". The killer phrase was "those words would make a weasel blush". Two months later, *The Times* said that Cameron was "being tipped as the man to watch".

But then, of course, from his contacts at Eton and Oxford, he has lots of friends in the press. The story was that the twenty-five-year-old Cameron was to replace Judith Chaplin as the Prime Minister's political secretary. In the end, the job went to Jonathan Hill, an older and more experienced pair of hands.

Instead Cameron was to brief John Major and Conservative Party Chairman Chris Patten for their daily press conferences in the run-up to the 1992 general election. It was, he said, a "pretty hairy job". Working up to twenty hours a day, he was one of the "brat pack" of young party strategists who slept in the "bunker", the headquarters of the campaign in a rented house in Gayfere Street, a stone's through from Central Office. The job had its dangers.

"I vividly remember being pinned to the wall and screamed at by Alastair Campbell, then political editor of the *Daily Mirror*, after the Conservatives' afternoon press conference," said Cameron. "I'm still waiting for my campaign medal from John Major."

He got into another fight with a member of his own party, Energy Secretary John Wakeham, for tinkering with quotes in a press release. Cameron was accused of being "at best cavalier... at worst contemptuous of the truth".

Cross words were also exchanged with John Major and, strangely, Cameron's name does not even appear in the index to John Major's autobiography. This is all the more peculiar when you consider that Cameron briefed him for PMQs twice a week for a year.

In the end, starting work each day at 4.45 in the morning proved too much for Cameron. Having been passed over for the job of political secretary, he said he had decided to quit politics and pursue a career in journalism.

To Cameron's surprise, the Conservatives won the 1992 election. Nevertheless, the brat pack seized the opportunity to break out the champagne. They then trooped across the Smith Square to the Labour headquarters, Transport House, to jeer at the losers, before continuing the revelry at Maurice Saatchi's house.

The following day, there was more triumphalism from "Chris Patten's babes". *The Times* reported: "Having been universally blamed for the Tories' lacklustre campaign, they felt vindicated as they opened yet another bottle of champagne at Conservative party headquarters. David Cameron , aged 25, an Old Etonian, said: 'The brat pack hits back.' Mr Cameron, who briefed John Major and the party chairman twice a day, said: 'Whatever people say about us, we got the campaign right.'"

But along the way Cameron had damaged his standing in the party.

Tory grandee Lord McAlpine wrote: "I do not know Mr Cameron and from what I hear of him I have no desire to. It is tempting to put these appalling creatures out of one's mind."

The former Tory party treasurer went on to remark on his "obvious arrogance", adding: "If Cameron were a dentist, I'm not sure I'd let him touch my teeth."

Nevertheless, Cameron could not help congratulating himself. In his campaign headquarters, he had a scorecard that read: "Played one, won one."

Despite his vow to quit politics, Cameron was hooked. He was given a job as special advisor to the Chancellor of the Exchequer Norman Lamont, who considered him too young. But with Britain's economic woes, Lamont had not been having a happy time in Number Eleven. Things got worse when it came out that he had inadvertently let his Notting Hill flat to sex therapist Lindi St Clair, aka Miss Whiplash. He badly needed a PR make-over and Number Ten decided that Cameron was just the man to do it.

His new colleagues, including Lamont's Chief Secretary Michael Portillo, were impressed. But Portillo added a caveat: "I have heard he is not, sometimes, as nice in private as you might think."

With the election behind him, Cameron took time to relax at Oxfordshire shooting parties. He was seen smoking a cigar and sporting red braces, popular with Big Bang bankers at the time. He took up playing bridge, running a school in the £130,000 flat he bought in Notting Hill. He also obtained a battered white BMW, which he drove to work.

With the affair with Laura Adshead behind him, he was now a free agent and journalist Petronella Wyatt, daughter of ex-MP and political columnist Woodrow Wyatt, went weak at the knees over him. They met at a party at Number Eleven.

"He had me in his arms. His breath was warm on my face. Oh, be still my beating heart! It all lasted less than an hour, but I shall never forget," she said.

Some thirteen years later, after her much publicized affair with Boris Johnson had ended, she looked back on that moment of bliss with Dave, sighing ruefully: "He touched the floor with the grace of Astaire and the manliness of Gene Kelly. Why did I muff my chance to become wife of the next Conservative Party leader?"

Cameron was in Number Eleven on Black Wednesday where the pound fell out of the European Exchange Rate Mechanism at a cost of £3.3 million. In the run-up to the crash, he found himself in a difficult position. When John Major was Mrs Thatcher's Chancellor, he had taken the pound into the ERM. Lamont, though, was not an enthusiast. It was Cameron's job to negotiate the diverging opinions of the two men. He did this with characteristic shrewdness.

"He's not rabidly ideological," said Michael Gove. "He is the kind of poker player who waits and reads the other players and bets when he knows the alignment is in his favour."

Nor did the impending crisis worry him.

"He never has sleepless nights," Gove continued. "He cooks to unwind or watches nature programmes, he is passionate about his vegetable patch and, on holiday, he likes going swimming in freezing cold water."

Indeed as the ERM began to creak, he took a holiday with friends, then one with his family. Then, when he came back, he was seen dining in the three-star Michelin restaurant with old flame Laura Adshead. Indeed, Lamont described Cameron as "a brilliant old Etonian with a taste for the good life".

He was certainly cool in the crisis that would end his boss's political career.

"Just before Black Wednesday he bought me a cigar a foot long and said, 'by the time you have smoked all of this all your troubles will be over'," Lamont recalled. "I have never smoked it."

On the day itself, with David Cameron famously hovering in the background and interest rates rocketing to twelve per cent, Norman Lamont had to announce in the words of his political advisor: "Today has been an extreme difficult and turbulent day. I will be reporting to the Cabinet and discussing the situation with colleagues tomorrow."

That night, Cameron called, telling Lamont cheerily: "There is good news and bad news, Chancellor. The good news is that your picture is on the front page of the *Sun*. The bad news is that it's in the middle of a dartboard."

Lamont acknowledged that Cameron gave him "a lot of invaluable help" over the speech that he had to make at the party conference in Brighton afterwards. Nevertheless, Cameron was in an unenviable position as the tension continued to grow between the Chancellor and the PM. And Lamont had not made things any easier for himself by telling a journalist that his wife had heard him singing in the bath just four days after Black Wednesday.

Matters did not improve when the *Sun* hacked into Lamont's credit card account and discovered that the Chancellor had gone over his credit limit twenty-two times in the previous eight years. "Threshergate" followed. The press reported that Lamont had bought a bottle of cut-price champagne and twenty Raffles cigarettes from a branch of Threshers in a seedy part of Paddington. While Lamont ignored the story, Cameron had to handle the press.

Lending a hand at the Newbury by-election, Lamont lunched with the Camerons at the Old Rectory in Peasemore. Out canvassing afterwards, he was asked by the BBC's John Pienaar: "Chancellor, which do you regret most, seeing green shoots or singing in the bath?"

"*Je ne regrette rien,*" quipped Lamont. Cameron was thought to have been responsible for the Chancellor stealing Edith Piaf's line. It was Lamont's death knell. He was blamed for the loss of the by-election and sacked.

With the fall of Norman Lamont, Cameron was out of a job too. Strings were pulled around Whitehall. Most ministers were reluctant to take him on. However, Michael Howard, who had known him from his days at the Conservative research department, gave Cameron a job in the Home Office, where he became a special advisor to a junior minister. There, it was all hands to the pumps as the Conservatives were in retreat in the face of Shadow Home

Secretary Tony Blair's oft-repeated mantra: "Tough on crime, tough on the causes of crime."

Cameron was also asked to use his influence with Lamont to stop him using his resignation speech to attack John Major, the way Geoffrey Howe had used his to bring down Margaret Thatcher only three years earlier. He failed and Lamont holed Major's government below the waterline, claiming they were "in office, but not in power".

He found himself further out of favour when Howard's name was added to Major's list of "bastards" and Laura Adshead, aka Miss Maastricht, became one of Major's most senior advisors on Europe. So Cameron had to abandon any suspicion of Euro-scepticism and distance himself from his former boss. At the next party conference, Lamont said: "I saw David Cameron, my former special advisor at the Treasury, who cut me dead."

This was not the first time in Cameron's career that he was seen as ruthless.

He got some of the credit for Howard's response to Blair's assault with "prison works". Meanwhile Major was foundering with "back to basics". This invited ridicule. Soon civil servants were jealously complaining that the Home Office had become a PR machine for Howard, who only "talks to young public school gentlemen from the party headquarters".

Cameron was at work behind the scenes too as a member of a dining club run by the deputy editor of the *Sunday Times*, Martin Ivens. It was called the Fellow Travellers and met at the Travellers

Club to discuss the issues of the day. Journalist Anne McElvoy recalled Cameron at a dinner in honour of John Redwood "flushed with excitement, shirt hanging out and waving a large cigar while talking very tough about free markets".

At the time, Cameron was known to be on the hard-right. Introduced to Enoch Powell, he spoke of privatizing the prison service. This was too much for Powell, who considered the penal system the duty of the state.

As well as calling for stiffer sentences, Cameron also wanted to liberalized the licensing laws.

"Licensing has long been a favourite topic of mine," he said. "When at the Home Office as a special adviser in the early 1990s, I wrote endless papers about scrapping our ludicrous laws. The permanent secretary, who was also tiring of my missives about stiff minimum sentences for burglars, summoned me to his office and said: 'Cameron, as far as I can see you want half the population in prison and the other half in the pub.'"

However, when Cameron actually visited a prison, he was shocked and his views became more humane.

Howard found himself in hot water when he tried to sack Derek Lewis, head to the prison service. Cameron was sent to talk to Lewis, though failed to keep a lid on the ensuing row. There was more trouble when Cameron was attacked for leaking the story of a meeting between Major and Labour leader John Smith. However, he managed to help stitch up a deal over so-called 'video nasties' with Tony Blair, meeting the future Prime Minister for the first time.

Despite these ups and downs, Cameron got on candidates' list at Smith Square in 1994. It seemed likely that he would be found a safe seat. Then John Smith died suddenly and Cameron knew his political fortunes had changed. The Conservatives would be facing Tony Blair at the next election.

Chapter Five – Sam Cam

David Cameron's future wife Samantha Sheffield was a school friend of his sister Clare, and was in many ways even more posh that he was. She is the elder daughter of Sir Reginald Sheffield, 8th Baronet, a descendant of Charles II, and Annabel Jones, a businesswoman and socialite who was similarly well-connected. Her family was like something out of a Nancy Mitford novel.

An authentic Tory toff, Sir Reginald was an Old Etonian who can trace his bloodline back to the Knights Templar and the Fifth Crusade, and was president of the Brigg and Goole Conservative Association. Like Cameron's father, he was a member of White's. Other members include Prince Charles and Prince William.

After Samantha's younger sister Emily was born, her parents divorced, though remained friendly. At weekends at the former family seat Normanby Hall, Annabel would book two tables at a nearby restaurant – one for the family; one for the chauffeur. Later, Annabel remarried. Her second husband was William Waldorf Astor III, nephew of her own stepfather Michael Langhorne Astor. For five years, Viscount Astor was a minister in John Major's government and was richer by far than Cameron's multi-millionaire dad.

Samantha said she grew up "near Scunthorpe", referring to the 3,000 acres of arable land in north Lincolnshire that her father inherited, along with Thealby Hall. The main family seat, Normanby

Hall, was leased to Lincolnshire council in lieu of death duties, though the family retained accommodation there. And her father inherited Sutton Park, a £5-million mansion near York with another thousand acres, in 1997. The family had once owned Buckingham House, which was sold off and remodelled as Buckingham Palace, though the Sheffields held on to the furniture.

At the age of eleven, Samantha went to St Helen's, an independent school in Abingdon. In the holidays, she and her sister would help out at her mother's jewellery shop in Knightsbridge.

Samantha first met David when Clare had a party at Peasemore.

"Sam thought, 'Who's this crashing bore who is my friend's older brother?'" said Cameron of his first encounter with his future wife. She was "a sulky sixteen-year-old".

That autumn she moved to Marlborough College, where she took her A levels, and where she dressed as a Goth. Then she took a foundation course at Camberwell College of Arts before going on to study Fine Art at Bristol Polytechnic. There, she tried to shake off her aristocratic upbringing by getting a dolphin tattoo on her ankle, and hanging out with the likes of the musician and actor Adrian Thaws, known as Tricky, who was heavily into drugs.

In 1992, she was invited to holiday with the Camerons in Tuscany. It was then that romance bloomed, even though with her penchant for roll-your-own cigarettes and hippy interest in pop concerts as well as her youth – she was twenty-two to his twenty-seven – she did not fit the obvious profile of a Prime Minister's wife. What's more, he seemed rather serious compared with her bohemian friends, who found the idea that anyone would belong to the Conservative Party faintly ridiculous.

Nevertheless she was soon spending the night at his Notting Hill flat. One of the first stories Elliott and Hanning tell of their courtship is of the phone ringing one Sunday morning and Samantha calling from the bed: "If that's Norman Lamont, tell him to fuck off."

Other weekends, he would drive down to Bristol. Her drug-taking friends were unimpressed. He even got lost trying to find her flat in one of the seedier parts of Bristol and found himself asking directions from a prostitute. The influence of Samantha had the effect of liberalizing him, which immediately brought him into conflict with his boss. At the time Michael Howard was out to ban "raves"; Samantha was a fan.

The relationship was not intellectually challenging. Cameron was a fan of Ian Fleming. Although he had also read Rider Haggard and all of Graham Greene, he generally preferred movies – citing *Lawrence of Arabia* as his favourite, though he had watched *Where Eagles Dare* seventeen times. *Porridge* was his favourite sitcom and his musical taste was mainstream. After a friend took him to the Richard Strauss opera *Die Frau ohne Schatten*, they received a note a few days later, thanking them for "introducing him to Nation Socialism", with the last two words crossed and replaced with "the operas of Richard Strauss".

After visiting the family at Sutton Park, a pair of his underpants, washed and ironed, were returned to him by post with a note from

Samantha's formidable grandmother Nancie, saying: "You left these behind, and not in your room."

From the beginning, Cameron made it clear that he wanted to be an MP. Samantha had no knowledge of politics. She did not know that "One-Nation" Conservatism, originally coined by Benjamin Disraeli, refers to the socially conscious centrist wing of the party.

"I may not have read history at Oxbridge, but I know as much about politics as most people and it means nothing to me," she said.

But while she had no desire to be the wife of a politician, she embraced the role. In the summer of 1993, back in Tuscany, they had to entertain the Lamonts, playing endless games of bridge. Senior journalists were also on the guest list. As a result, Cameron's name was back in the papers.

At the Wyatts' Italian holiday home, Woodrow tried to persuade the women to go skinny-dipping in the pool. Guest Robin Day, the famous broadcaster, was particularly keen. Afterwards Samantha asked who that "dirty old man" had been. When informed, she said she had not recognized him without his bow tie.

In 1994, Samantha and David became secretly engaged. Cameron then told Michael Howard that he wanted to take a job outside politics. Conservative associations mark candidates down if they have not had a job outside politics. Besides, if he was to marry, he needed more money.

Samantha was not so sure about getting hitched. She was still rather young and her mother's first marriage had ended in divorce. But when Cameron sold his flat, she came up with some money and they bought their first home together – again in North Kensington – for £215,000. It was valued at over £1.5 million when he moved into Downing Street.

She also helped him get a well-paid job. He mother Lady Astor had a word with her friend Michael Green, chairman of Carlton Television, who hired Cameron as director of corporate affairs, the only job he has ever held outside politics. Green tried to makes it a proviso that Cameron would not fight the next election. Cameron would not agree to this, taking a lesser position at a lower salary – though still nearly twice what he had been earning at the Home Office.

Sam and Dave's engagement was announced in Nigel Dempster's society column in the *Daily Mail* in October 1994. The engagement was a long one. In March 1996, they had one final holiday as an unmarried couple in the West Indies, returning to make preparations for their nuptials in earnest.

Cameron's stag do involved an afternoon at the races. This was followed by a lavish dinner for thirty guests outdoors in a marquee. There were no strippers.

David and Samantha married on 1 June 1996 at the Church of St. Augustine of Canterbury, East Hendred, Oxfordshire. It rained heavily. One of the wedding photos shows the bride as her customary composed and sunny self, while tears stream down the groom's face. The wedding was a political affair with Michael Howard, Norman Lamont, Michael Green and the Duke of Westminster in attendance. There was little doubt among the guests that, despite her reckless youth, Sam Cam would make the perfect political wife.

By then she had given up her ambition to be a painter. She became an interior designer and professional window dresser, working four days a week as creative director of Smythson, the upmarket stationers in New Bond Street. It was a job again secured through family connections.

As a director of the company she said she earned more than her husband, whose salary when he rose to be Leader of the Opposition was £130,000 a year. But then money was not the issue. At one point, the compiler of the *Sunday Times* Rich List Philip Beresford valued the Tory leader for the first time.

He said: "I put the combined family wealth of David and Samantha Cameron at £30 million plus. Both sides of the family are extremely wealthy. They certainly have no need to worry about poverty or paying school fees."

By then they had three children – Nancy Gwen, born 2004; Arthur Elwen, born 2006 and disabled Ivan, born 2002. He suffered from cerebral palsy, complicated with severe epilepsy, and died in 2009.

In one interview, David Cameron mentioned that his wife "owns a field in Scunthorpe". That may not sound like much, but her father has been heard to say: "I live off unearned income, garnished by the occasional planning consent." In 2007, he was estimated to be worth £20 million.

Now a married man, Cameron buckled down to his day job. He said he admired Michael Green as a "swashbuckling entrepreneur".

He was one of Mrs Thatcher's favourite businessmen. But during his time at Carlton, the company faced a barrage of criticism over the low standards of its shows. Cameron's role was to handle the PR. He was to be the acceptable face of Carlton. It was an impossible task.

Financial journalist Jeff Randall, who has been business editor of virtually every heavyweight newspaper, along with the BBC and Sky, had many dealings with Cameron when he was head of communications at Carlton.

"I wouldn't trust him with my daughter's pocket money," he said. "In my experience, he never gave a straight answer when dissemblance was a plausible alternative. Whether he flat-out lied I won't say, but he went a long way to leave me with the impression that the story was wrong. He put up so much verbal tracker you started to lose your own guidance system."

Randall was not alone in this opinion among business journalists. Chris Blackhurst, City editor of the London *Evening Standard* said Cameron was "aggressive, sharp-tongued, often condescending and patronizing. If anyone had told me then he might become premier I would have told them to seek help."

Patrick Hosking, investment editor of *The Times*, said: "He was obstructive."

Most damning of all is this assessment by veteran City journalist Ian King, who called him "a poisonous, slippery individual," adding: "He was a smarmy bully who regularly threatened journalists. He loved humiliating people, including a colleague at ITV he would abuse publicly as 'Bunter', just because the poor bloke was a few pounds overweight. He was a mouthpiece for that company's charmless chairman, Michael Green, who operated him the way Keith Harris works Orville."

This was, perhaps, not the greatest period of Cameron's life. But then, the tempestuous Green was notoriously difficult to work with. Cameron's immediate boss when he first started at Carlton had been headhunted for the position. She lasted just five weeks, allowing him to step into her shoes.

At Carlton, Cameron maintained his political connections. In 1995, Cameron set up a meeting between Green and the Shadow Chancellor Gordon Brown, telling Green that Brown was "going places". Off duty, Cameron hung out at the Met Bar, a celebrity haunt in Mayfair, or he would go gambling with his boss at the Portland Club. But Cameron was not a natural high roller, playing cautiously even though his losses were guaranteed by Green. They also travelled to the US frequently to make deals. To liven things up with people who did not know them, they would swap identities, with Cameron playing the role of cantankerous tycoon.

Otherwise, his job consisted of giving a "bollocking" to the press on behalf of his boss and lobbying for a change in the Broadcasting Act with his father-in-law, Viscount Astor, then a minister in the Department of National Heritage.

Chapter Six – The Search for a Seat

David Cameron's search for a parliamentary seat began in Ashford, Kent. At a preliminary meeting with the local Conservative Association, Samantha made the mistake of wearing a skirt with a revealing split which had to be safety-pinned at the last moment. Cameron made it to the shortlist. But on the day of the selection, he planned to take the train to the constituency. It was cancelled. Downing Street policy advisor Damien Green arrived on time and was selected.

Then David Cameron came within a whisper of scandal. Money had been stolen from clients' accounts by a young broker at Panmure Gordon, when Ian Cameron was still running the company. The culprit claimed the swindle was part of a botch operation by British intelligence. This had been communicated to the Home Office while David Cameron was working there. Fortunately, neither the involvement of Cameron senior or Cameron junior was mentioned in the court case.

In 1995, John Major confronted his critics, resigned as party leader and called a leadership election in a "back me or sack me" move. Cameron was still in the Westminster loop and told Chris Patten he thought that Michael Portillo should be the next leader. Patten was not convinced.

"He looked at me quizzically and said: 'I am not sure we are ready for a Spanish Prime Minister.' Rich really, for a Europhile," said Cameron.

After missing out on a couple of other seats, Cameron was selected for Stafford, a seat vacated by Euro-sceptic Bill Cash after boundary changes. Cameron rented a farmhouse there and spent weekends in the constituency. Samantha was on hand to put up posters, though in the week she was busy refitting Smythson in an effort to modernize the business.

In 1996, she launched the company's iconic *Fashion Diary*, which carried listings of all the most stylish shops, restaurants and hotels in London, Milan, Paris and New York, as well as the relevant fashion show dates. Its cult status was immediately assured when Meg Mathews bought twenty-two as Christmas presents for her supermodel best friends.

"We were putting gold-stamped initials on them for people like Kate Moss and Naomi Campbell," said Sam, "and the great thing was that they all carried on using them."

The revamped store also became fashionable. Madonna, Harvey Keitel, Catherine Zeta Jones, Liv Tyler, Stella McCartney and Gwyneth Paltrow all became regular customers.

By the time the Camerons returned from their honeymoon in France and Italy, Cameron's political prospects had dimmed. The Conservative government was on its last legs and Tony Blair seemed an unstoppable force. Seeing which way the wind was blowing, Michael Green began employing stalwarts of New Labour.

Cameron spent more time in the constituency, where Cash's majority of 10,900 no longer seemed so safe. As a special advisor to Norman Lamont, he had advocated raising taxes. As a prospective parliamentary candidate attending the party conference in 1996 though, he demanded they be slashed.

In *The Times* that Christmas, Michael Gove indulged in a game of "Fantasy Cabinet". After a period of Blair government, he said, a resurgent Euro-sceptic Tory party would be swept back into power with John Redwood as PM, Giles Brandreth as Minister for Fun and "1997 entrant David Cameron as Chief Secretary to the Treasury, youth would have its head".

It was not to be. With Cameron opposing joining the euro during the election campaign, it was easy to paint him as a Tory right-winger – just the sort the country wanted to see the back of. Nevertheless, family and friends turned up in the constituency to hand out leaflets. The Home Secretary came to endorse the candidate and claim that Labour would put 24p on the price of a pint. But somehow Cameron's campaign never really took off.

Local councillor David Kidney beat him with a 10.7 per cent swing to Labour. Cameron was bitterly disappointed. Sensing which way the vote was going, a lot of supporters deserted him before the returning officer announced the result. Even Sam Cam spent the night drinking the car park with the Monster Raving Loony Party, who had received a creditable 248 votes – though their candidate Aston A.N. May also claimed the large number of spoiled ballots, arguing that anyone who had spoilt their ballot must be a raving loony.

Later Cameron made light of it, saying: "On election night in 1997, when I crashed and burned as the Tory candidate in Stafford, an old lady came to me in tears and said: 'I don't want to die under a Labour government.' Perhaps there were thousands of others like her who didn't wait for the final results and took pre-emptive action."

Cameron returned to Carlton, which was now involved in takeover battles and a disastrous foray into digital broadcasting, ultimately losing out to Rupert Murdoch and Sky. There was a furore when the *Guardian* exposed a documentary on the cocaine trade which Carlton broadcast as a fake. The attack was so dire that Cameron dodged journalists' questions by claiming to the "John Smith". This valiant rear-guard action won him few friends in the press. He tried to bounce back, but even the charm offensive he organized backfired due to the feistiness of Green.

"I've had my fair share of media disasters," Cameron said. "Most of them occur either when you don't know the answer to a question, or when you do but can't say. As well as actually saying: 'I don't know' or 'I can't tell you', we've all tried variants such as 'I'll get back to you' and then leaving the phone off the hook, or roaring with laughter and saying 'who on earth told you that?' But the one thing even the lowliest of spin paramedics is taught is that you must not lie: it means the end of your credibility and it should mean the end of your job."

Some say, at Carlton, Cameron came perilously close to the mark, if not actually stepping over it. If caught out, he apologized. But at the behest of his boss, Cameron often found himself in the position where he had to defend the indefensible.

As the 2001 election approached, Cameron again began looking round for a winnable seat. He tried for Kensington and Chelsea after the death of Alan Clark in 1999, but did not make the shortlist.

In Wealdon in Sussex, he was in the final two, but lost out to ex-MP Charles Hendry who had lived in the constituency since he was eight.

"Cameron should have slaughtered him," insiders told the *Guardian*'s Michael White.

In April 2000 Cameron was selected for Witney in Oxfordshire over Andrew Mitchell, who was accused of sleaze although he had been cleared. It had been a safe Conservative seat but sitting MP Shaun Woodward, who had worked with Cameron on the 1992 election campaign, had defected to Labour. Mitchell was returned for Sutton Coldfield and rose to become Cameron's Chief Whip, before falling from power in "Plebgate".

By this time, in selection meetings, Cameron had learnt to speech fluently without notes, a technique that would stand him in good stead later in his career. This new approach had been Samantha's idea.

The president of the local Conservative Association, Lord Chadlington, offered them a cottage on his estate at Dean, and Cameron went to work right away nursing his constituency.

That December, Cameron turned his fire on his former friend Shaun Woodward, with the letter in the *Daily Telegraph* suggesting that he had made an "unprincipled U-turn" on hunting to sway selection committees in safe Labour seats. Cameron also seized the opportunity to distance himself from "the issue that triggered his resignation – Clause 28 and the promotion of homosexuality in schools". It was a theme Cameron would return to, though in 2013 he backed the bill allowing gay marriage.

On the stump, a local pointed out the pub where the police arrested British Union of Fascist leader Oswald Mosley in 1940, saying: "Apparently Shaun Woodward drinks there now."

"I made some cheap crack about 'the police not bothering to arrest traitors these days' and went on my way," said Cameron.

In 2001, the election was delayed for a month due to an outbreak of foot-and-mouth, so Cameron undertook a sponsored bicycle ride around all eighty-five parishes in the Witney constituency. Covering 220 miles in five days, he raised £4,000 for charity.

"My local Conservative agent is still chuckling," said Cameron. "He applauded my determination, but worries about my naivety: not knowing that 'bike' is slang for prostitute, my press release announcing this caper opened with the quote: 'I haven't been on a bike for years.' Looking back, I can see his point."

Seeing his old headmaster, Eric Anderson, in the street, Cameron ran after him shouting: "Sir, Sir, will you vote for me?"

Cameron took the fight onto enemy territory with a column on the website *Guardian Unlimited* where he called the Labour candidate "one of those I-feel-your-pain, rock-crushing bores" and the Liberal a "human-hamster cross".

Still, he sought inspiration from far and wide.

"There is an iconic figure from the 1970s and 1980s that should inspire the Conservative party this week," he wrote "I am of course referring to the hairy godfather of punk rock who recently died of cancer, Joey Ramone."

Then there was the visit to a medical supplies company in his constituency.

"It markets a new machine called the Rapport, the full description of which is a 'vacuum therapy device for erectile dysfunction'. I will spare you the details (large test tube, small pump, painful looking rubber band)."

He also had some criticism of the electoral strategy of the party leader William Hague, who had focussed the election campaign on Europe and slashing the price of petrol.

"But will these two issues… remain high enough up the agenda to alter how people vote?" asked Cameron. "Knocking on doors in the evening, the answer would probably be no. Education and the NHS predominate, where battle honours are more evenly shared."

It seems he was right. The Conservatives lost the election, though Cameron won his seat and was on his way to parliament.

Chapter Seven – The Greasy Pole

As soon as Cameron arrived in the House of Commons, he had to decide who to back in the leadership election. For a moment, he even considered standing himself, but quickly realized it was too soon.

Nevertheless, a week after being elected, he set out his stall. He told the *Daily Telegraph*: "Millwall fans used to be proud of the fact that 'nobody likes us; we don't care'. The Conservative Party must not fall into the same trap. It has to change its language, change its approach, start with a blank sheet of paper and try to work out why our base of support is not broader. Anyone could have told the Labour Party in the 1980s how to become electable. It had to drop unilateral disarmament, punitive tax rises, wholesale nationalization and unionization. The question for the Conservative Party is far more difficult because there are no obvious areas of policy that need to be dropped. We need a clear, positive, engaging agenda on public services."

Two weeks later, Cameron's name appeared on a list of possible Portillo backers, in the belief that he was going to win.

The parliamentary sketch writers could not wait for Cameron's maiden speech as there was a tradition in the House of praising one's predecessor. He did this with characteristic deftness. Woodward, he said, "remains a constituent, and a most significant local employer, not least in the area of domestic service…" As a Labour candidate,

Woodward had taken stick over the fact that he had a butler, courtesy of his wife, supermarket heiress Camilla Sainsbury.

"We are in fact quite close neighbours," Cameron continued. "On a clear day, from the hill behind my cottage, I can almost see some of the glittering spires of his great house."

His mother watched the speech on the parliamentary channel and phoned up to say: "You need a haircut to stop looking like Peter Mandelson, don't wave your arms around while speaking and tell the man behind you to stop picking his nose."

In the first round of the leadership ballot, Portillo was eliminated.

"The Spanish armada goes down with all hands, including this particular new boy," rued Cameron. "Our man had offered leadership, radical change and ideas that challenged the party both in parliament and the country. They simply weren't ready for it. In many ways it is a view I share."

In the second round, Cameron voted for the winner Iain Duncan Smith over Ken Clarke because, he said: "Mr Clarke's saloon bar habit of calling his opponents 'head bangers' or 'hangers and floggers' always gives me the shivers... Mr Clarke's man-of-the-people, broad-brush approach has minuses as well as pluses. As a former adviser put it to me years ago: 'The trouble with Ken's broad brush is that everyone else gets splattered with paint.'" It was, of course, Kenneth Clarke who had lost him his job at the Treasury when he took over from Norman Lamont.

Cameron was immediately appointed to the prestigious Home Affairs Select Committee, a showcase for new talent. The first thing he suggested was that look into the problems of heroin addiction or changing the law on cannabis.

"On the drugs issue, I am an instinctive liberal (small l, please), disliking state bans on anything," he said, "but my worry has always been the very simple point that legalization will make drugs more available and more people will try them."

Home Secretary David Blunkett responded by downgrading cannabis from being a Class B drug to Class C. Cameron then attacked him for not going far enough. The committee eventually recommended that Ecstasy be downgraded from Class A to Class B and the trial of "shooting galleries" where addicts could inject heroin.

Assessing the new crop of MPs in *The Times*, Michael Gove said: "Media attention, so far, has inevitably concentrated on the biggest body in the firmament – the hulking, shaggy form of Boris Johnson, *Spectator* editor and MP for Henley. Johnson's undoubted writing talent, combined with a hairstyle like a Tongan's skirt and a voice genetically designed to instil fear in Pathan tribesmen, commands attention. But the Commons tends to be suspicious of those who have enjoyed conspicuous success before entering and Boris may have to tread carefully to ensure that his talents flourish. Behind Johnson, however, there are several others who may be the Blairs, Browns or even Mandelsons of their generation. Noticeable so far are David Cameron, the MP for Witney, Mark Field (Cities of London and Westminster), Mark Francois (Rayleigh), Paul Goodman (Wycombe), and George Osborne (Tatton)... Cameron brings all the professionalism and sophistication to politics of one who has worked in both Whitehall and television…."

Following the 9/11 attacks in New York and Washington, David Blunkett introduced the Anti-Terrorism, Crime and Security Bill which had to be debated line-by-line on the floor of the house. Knowing this would attract media attention, both Cameron and Osborne sat in the chamber throughout. They lived near to each other and Osborne would give Cameron a lift home, before they both began cycling.

Cameron was determined to raise his profile. In the *Guardian*, he admitted to being "a media tart. I spent a large portion of the last week negotiating with, preparing for and appearing on radio and television programmes."

He was on Radio Four's *Any Questions*, Channel Four's *Richard and Judy*, with a walk-on part in BBC One's *Crimewatch* in between.

He also confessed: "When a politician turns his back on the mother of parliaments and heads for the studio lights, the green room and the powder puff, the excuses start to flow. 'I need the practice'. 'It is important to use the media to communicate'. And the very self-serving: 'How can I change the world if no one knows who I am?' I fully admit to rehearsing all three."

He had some advice to share when it came to appearing on *Any Questions*: "My tips are: don't drink anything at the dinner with Jonathan Dimbleby before the show; don't worry about the audience in the hall baying for your blood – concentrate on the folks at home.

And try to sound reasonable. Michael Portillo once told me a tip he had been given: by being thoroughly rude and aggressive to the other panellists at the dinner you can wind them up in to fits of indignation. They will then rant and rave on air and you will come over cool as the proverbial cucumber."

His tip for television appearances was to promise the producer a right-wing rant, then say something more reasonable when you are on air, read the schedules beforehand and have some jokes ready.

In the House, as a countryman, Cameron got the bit between his teeth about the hunting ban, heckling Ann Widdecombe and calling Gerald Kaufman a "pompous prat". He took to riding to hounds in his constituency. He also stalked deer and went fly-fishing on Jura where the Astors had a house. There he swam in the sea every day before dinner, whatever the weather, and has been known to take a dip in an icy brook when a guest at other country estates.

He supported Tony Blair over the interventions in both Afghanistan and Iraq.

"I am an instinctive hawk about these things," he said. "Everyone knows that Saddam is a monster."

However, he admitted to being "confused and uncertain" about it. In the end, though, he voted for the invasion of Iraq "grudgingly, unhappily, unenthusiastically". Nevertheless, he gave praise where praise was due.

"Blair himself has been masterful," he said after the vote. "It pains me to say so, but it's true. The speech in the great debate was a parliamentary triumph and it would be churlish to deny it. I've even sent copies to constituents writing to me about the war."

But in the long run he foresaw problems for both parties: "A long, unpopular war ending Blair's reign... Conservatives tainted with support for the government's war."

Iain Duncan Smith's leadership of the Conservative Party did not go well. In November 2002, he sent for Cameron, Osborne and Boris Johnson to help him brush up his performance at PMQs. But while remaining a key advisor, Cameron found he could not support his leader in a key vote on allowing gay and unmarried couples adopt. At the time, Cameron was having problems on his own, spending nights in hospital with Ivan. Though he appeared gaunt and tired to those around him, the *Sunday Times* were soon tipping Cameron as future Tory Prime Minister.

By February 2003, Conservative MPs were petitioning for a vote of no confidence in IDS. Then, after the local elections in May, Crispin Blunt, the Shadow Secretary of State for Trade and Industry resigned, calling Duncan Smith's leadership a "handicap".

Cameron remained in the inner circle and he was made deputy shadow Leader of the House. This gave him his first chance to get to the despatch box. At first, he was thrown by the sledging of the veteran Labour bruiser Dennis Skinner. But then he got into his stride.

Quentin Letts noted in the *Daily Mail*: "This was the best parliamentary debut I have seen."

However, Cameron was nervous of articles saying that he was destined for high office, especially when written by friends. He told a local paper: "It's very flattering but often something like this signals the end of your political career rather than the beginning."

In October, a vote of no confidence was called. In private, Cameron advised Duncan Smith to stand down rather than risk a humiliating defeat. He voted for his leader anyway, but Duncan Smith lost and was replaced by Michael Howard.

Throughout the early years of David Cameron's parliamentary career, he and Samantha had to cope with a severely ill child. He had missed two party conferences to be at Ivan's bedside. In late 2003, he began to talk about it publicly as the Labour government's policy of integrating disabled children into mainstream schools threatened Ivan's day-care centre. What's more, Ivan's condition was deteriorating. He was losing even the capacity to smile.

While admitting it was illogical, Ivan's terrible plight made Cameron more religious.

"Obviously I pray for him," he said. "The truth is the first person who says 'some good will come of this' you want to thump really quite hard, but actually some good does come of even terrible things like that."

Despite the hardship at home, there was still a political battle to fight. On taking office Howard appointed Cameron as deputy chairman of the Conservative Party, then secretly asked him to embarrass the government by preparing a briefing on the Hutton Inquiry that was looking into the circumstances surrounding the death of Dr David Kelly, who had supposedly told BBC journalist Andrew Gilligan that Tony Blair's dossier outlining the causes for invading Iraq had been "sexed up". Somehow the nature of this task was leaked to the papers.

Cameron's report, condemning Blair, was published a few weeks before Lord Hutton's – which unexpectedly exonerated Blair and condemned the BBC. Howard had no choice but to accept Hutton's conclusions before a howling House. Cameron's punishment was to go on *Newsnight*, where he waffled, prompting Jeremy Paxman to ask: "What are you wittering on about?"

Howard tried to make some political capital out of the situation by saying that he would not have voted to go to war if he had known what he knew now, while Cameron reverted to his original position, saying it was right to support the US and the UN, and get rid of Saddam Hussein. A struggle ensued, with Howard abandoning the script that Cameron had prepared for PMQs and demanding that Blair apologize for misleading the country over the weapons of mass destruction Saddam was supposed to have had.

In March 2004, Cameron was appointed "spokesman on local government finance and council tax". Though the local elections were due in June, it seemed he was being sidelined. With the question of Europe top of the agenda, Cameron began holding secret talks with anti-EU campaigners.

The party was growing disillusioned with Howard, and David Davis was tipped to succeed him. But others were already grooming

Cameron. He had even been sounded out to run for the leadership before Duncan Smith had fallen.

In the summer of 2003, Cameron himself began to gather his forces. He persuaded *Times* columnist Michael Gove to stand for parliament. After a period out of politics, his old friend from the Conservative research department Steve Hilton had returned as special advisor to Maurice Saatchi, who Howard had appointed party chairman. He too got himself on the candidates' list.

In the spring of 2004, Gove held the first of a series of dinners in a Mayfair restaurant to start planning what should happen after the 2005 election where defeat seemed likely. Over the following year, these dinners transferred to Cameron's home in Finstock Road, North Kensington. Many of those who attended were from Howard's inner office.

In July 2004, a call went out that "bed-blockers" – Tory MPs in their fifties and sixties holding safe seats – should step aside for young Turks. Veteran MP Derek Conway responded by pointing the finger at Cameron and his cronies.

"This is what we call the Notting Hill Tory set," he said. "They sit around in these curious little bistros in parts of London, drink themselves silly and wish they were doing what the rest of us are getting on with. They'll just have to be a little more patient."

The following day the newspapers carried maps showing where area where the members lived. Hilton told the *Guardian*: "There is no point in pretending. We are mates. We go on holiday and have been doing this for years. We all worked together at Conservative

Central Office in the run up to the 1992 election. That was the origin of the friendship."

One of those named was Rachel Whetstone, who had been at the Conservative research department and was then political secretary to Michael Howard. She was also thought to be Hilton's on-again, off-again lover and the couple were Ivan's godparents.

As interest peaked, Richard Kay wrote in the *Daily Mail*: "There is, I can reveal today, an intriguing romantic spring in the step of Rachel Whetstone, Tory leader Michael Howard's political secretary and queen bee of the so-called Notting Hill set of bright young Conservatives. The Benenden-educated brunette, who is one of Mr Howard's two most senior special advisers, has, I understand, formed a close friendship with a married older man who is a well-connected Tory grandee."

Kay then gave an intriguing hint of who the grandee might be.

"In her role as political adviser, one figure Miss Whetstone has helped promote is David Cameron, 37, the Conservative MP for Witney in Oxfordshire and a happily married father-of-two (with whom she is not involved romantically). Eton-educated Cameron, who is in charge of policy co-ordination for the party, is the stepson-in-law of Viscount Astor, 52, a former government whip and Opposition spokesman in the House of Lords. William Astor lives with his wife Annabel and their three children in a Jacobean manor house in rural Oxfordshire."

Whetstone then confessed she was having an affair with Astor. Cameron was furious for the sake of both his mother-in-law Annabel and his close friend Hilton. The situation was all the more awkward because he was policy co-ordinator and a member of the shadow cabinet. Consequently, he needed regular access to Howard and his advisors.

Cameron was now to take the lead in putting across Tory party policy with articles in the newspapers and an appearance on *Question Time*. He was then put in charge of writing the manifesto for the 2005 election. It seemed to some that Howard was anointing Cameron as his successor. However, colleagues were miffed when, in the run-up to the election, Cameron seemed to distance himself from both the leadership and their policies. Which was just as well. Although the Conservatives gained thirty-three seats, this only put a small dent in the massive Labour majority. Afterwards, Michael Howard decided that, at sixty-three, he was simply too old to fight another election and would stand down.

Chapter Eight – Race for the Leadership

Michael Howard did not want David Davis to succeed him, and Rachel Whetstone persuaded him to delay his resignation long enough for Cameron and Osborne to prepare a challenge. To give him a leg up, Howard offered Cameron the prestigious position of Shadow Chancellor. He refused, not wanting to have to take on Gordon Brown in the House. Instead he became Shadow Education Secretary. George Osborne became Shadow Chancellor instead.

There had been another motive behind Cameron's refusal of the Shadow Chancellorship. He and Osborne had long been dubbed the Blair and Brown of the Conservative Party. But which was which? Being the older, more experienced man, Cameron feared comparison to Brown. Brown had been Shadow Chancellor under John Smith, only to find himself trumped by Blair who had a weaker position as Shadow Home Secretary, not Labour's strong suit. When Cameron heard that Osborne had accepted the position as Shadow Chancellor, he punched the air.

Howard now switched his support to Osborne, thinking he had a better chance to beat David Davis. Meanwhile Cameron was telling the press that he had no ambitions to be leader and still had faith in Howard, though Gove said this was not disingenuous. Cameron was simply "playing his cards close to his chest". However, privately, his parents and, particularly, Samantha were urging him to run. The decision was made in the garden at Dean.

"I remember walking around talking to Sam and thinking right, 'Come on'," he said. "She took the view, look, the Conservative party needs to change, get on and do it."

Osborne decided not to run. As the younger man, he could afford to wait.

"There was no Granita moment," said Cameron – Granita being the name of the Islington restaurant when it was agreed that Blair would run for the leadership of the Labour party after the death of John Smith and Brown would succeed him. However, there were long telephone conversations between Cameron and Osborne before the decision was taken, and Osborne agreed to become Cameron's campaign manager. They both knew that there was one issue that they would have to address in the contest. That was class.

"Am I too posh to push?" Cameron asked in the *Observer*. "In the sort of politics I believe in it shouldn't matter what you've had in the past, it's what you are going to contribute in the future, and I think that should be true of everybody, from all parts of society, all colours and ages and races, and I hope that goes for Old Etonians too."

There had not been an Old Etonian Prime Minister since Sir Alec Douglas-Home in 1964. Home had been a friend of Cameron's grandfather, the 2nd Baronet, William Mount, when they had been at Oxford together.

After turning down the offer to be Kenneth Clarke's running mate, Cameron set about raising money. He had little support among the parliamentary party, but a bid to restrict the vote to MPs was defeated, so Cameron set about creating a buzz in the media and, by the time the competition got underway, the bookmakers were giving odds of five to one on him, making him second favourite behind Davis at evens, while Clarke was at ten to one.

The campaign did not start well, with Cameron making hardly a dent in Davis's lead among the party faithful. His support among MPs barely made it into double figures.

Cameron decided that the best strategy was to pretend that he had already won the leadership contest and was now out to win a general election. His slogan would be "modern compassionate conservatism" and set about buttering up the press. But while the political commentators were wowed, his support in the party was ebbing away. Osborne even accepted an invitation to a house party by Andrew Mitchell who was running David Davis's campaign. There were even calls for Cameron to pull out of the race.

Osborne was not convinced that Cameron could win, believing he was too much of a gentleman to be seen trying too hard. Indeed, when the going got tough, Cameron took a holiday. Even so, when he returned, he refused to do a deal with Davis.

A campaign office was set up in Greycoat Place, just round the corner from Conservative Party headquarters, and an extra £20,000 was raised from backers to launch the campaign on the same day that Davis was launching his. Going head to head with the frontrunner would give him more credibility as a contender.

The venue would be the Whitehall headquarters of the Royal United Services Institute. The journalists covering it had come direct from the Institute of Civil Engineers in Great George Street where Davis had launched his campaign in an oak panelled room.

"The launch was austere. No frills, no food," wrote Ann Treneman in *The Times*. "Dave's launch was just down the road but it seemed to be in another world."

She noted that Cameron had consciously rebranded himself as "Dave" to distinguish himself from David Davis.

"Dave even served us strawberry smoothies. Smoothies at a political launch! Whatever next? Aromatherapy?" Treneman said.

No oak panels here.

"The room was white and circular. The music was calming with lots of little chimes and bells and what-not. I am only surprised that we were not handed little white towels and lavender eye-pads... Even when Dave arrived, seriously late for his own party, the dream-like atmosphere continued. The words 'passionate' and 'caring' washed round us like waves lapping the beach. He kept saying: 'There's a we in politics as much as a me.' It could be his catchphrase because, even in a dream, it makes no sense."

Cameron was improvising. He had decided the day before to abandon the script and speak off the cuff.

Michael Howard had deliberately decided to stay on as leader until after the conference at Blackpool as part of this "stop Davis" strategy. This would give the various candidates the opportunity to parade their talents in a conference speech – something he knew Davis was not very good at.

Cameron was taken to a tailor to have a new suit made that cost over a thousand pounds, while Samantha visited the Marks and Spencers in Blackpool for a new pair of shoes and a selection of ties. Meanwhile Hilton bashed out a daily campaign newsletter that was distributed to delegates. A professional marketing man, he also gave out "I □ DC" badges. Davis countered with a big-breasted woman wearing a "It's DD for me" T-shirt.

In his conference speech Cameron again spoke without notes. It was a technique he had now mastered. The speech was a tour de force. It attacked Labour, recalled Margaret Thatcher, promised to "switch on a whole new generation to the Conservative Party" and ended: "If we go for it, if we seize it, if we fight for it with every ounce of passion, vigour and energy from now until the next election, nothing, and no one, can stop us."

There were twenty rounds of applause during the twenty-minute speech and he got a three-minute ovation, admittedly aided by his campaign team who had bagged the front seats. Then the heavily pregnant Samantha came on stage. He patted her on the stomach, giving the photographers a visual image of the new generation.

According to the BBC website, the best joke of the speech was: "It's not just about having a young, vigorous, energetic leader – although come to think of it, it's not such a bad idea." It was not so much of a joke though. Ken Clarke was sixty-five and his speech only got a two-minute ovation.

David Davis's ovation was just one-and-a-half minutes. Malcolm Rifkind said unkindly: "He must be very, very worried because he was speaking to a party of Conservative enthusiasts who wanted to will him to succeed. If he was unable to achieve that, one has to ask the question how would he deal with Gordon Brown over the next four years."

The *Sunday Telegraph* was also disappointed with Davis's performance.

"He should have ripped up his paper speech, stepped in front of the podium and congratulated Mr Cameron on his dazzling debut the day before," it said.

However, Cameron had another storm to weather. At a fringe meeting, journalist Andrew Rawnsley asked him if he had taken drugs at university. Cameron replied: "I had a normal university experience."

"So that's a yes then," said Rawnsley.

The newspapers then demanded that he come clean on drugs, but Cameron adopted the standard defence: "I did all sorts of things before I came into politics which I shouldn't have done. We all did."

The other candidates had no problem denying they had ever taken drugs, but Cameron could not because of his peccadillo at Eton. The *Daily Mail* wanted to know whether his own experiences were the cause of his liberal attitude to drugs.

"Nothing could be further from the truth," he said. "I've seen the dreadful damage that drugs can do."

The first round of voting, just two weeks after the conference, excluded Clarke, with Cameron coming just six votes behind Davis. The next round of voting excluded Liam Fox, putting Cameron ahead of Davis by thirty-three – though there were suspicions in the Fox camp that Cameron had persuaded some supporters to vote for Davis to keep their man out of second place. This was certainly discussed, though Cameron concluded that he could not vote against himself.

These preliminary rounds were among MPs. The two remaining candidates now had to go head-to-head in a ballot of the membership. This was where class became the crucial issue. Fellow MPs knew him for the man he was. But outsiders saw him as a man from a rich and privileged background who surrounded himself with other Old Etonians.

David Davis, on the other hand, was the son of a single mother who had been brought up on a council estate. He had worked as an insurance clerk and joined the Territorial Army's SAS regiment to support himself while he took his A levels. After that, he went to Warwick University, the London Business School and Harvard, before working for Tate & Lyle for seventeen years. This was a meritocratic background Cameron could not match.

But Cameron was a skilful politician who knew how to occupy the enemy's territory. He gave an interview to the *Sun*. In it, he cleverly played down his poshness.

He preferred a pint of real ale bitter or a glass of red wine to sipping champagne, he said, and both he and his wife were Skoda drivers, until thieves burgled his home in Notting Hill and drove off in one packed with their swag.

"The dad of two smokes Marlboro Lights and enjoys nights out at a 'spit and sawdust' tapas bar in the Portobello Road," the *Sun* said. "His favourite telly shows are *Desperate Housewives*, *Lost* and *Spooks*… The Jam and Bob Dylan were his rock idols as a teenager and now he's a fan of David Gray, James Blunt, Radiohead and The Killers. And he relaxes on a Saturday morning listening to Radio Two's Jonathan Ross while chopping logs."

He was an Aston Villa who did not think, just because he went to Eton, he was "born to rule". However, he did want to be Prime Minister, largely for his wife's sake.

"She's fed up with the Tories losing and doesn't want to be married to a Tory MP who loses elections all the time," he said.

How was he going to square up to Tony Blair and Gordon Brown?

"Blair is going to be irrelevant," he replied. "He's soon going to be off on his lecture tour of the USA, stopping only briefly at Cliff Richard's Barbados villa on the way."

While he was brought up in a wealthy family, Cameron insisted that he was not rich.

"I could not afford to send my kids to Eton," he said. What's more he did not own a private jet, or know anyone who did. "I would like my children to go to state schools if they can." Though he saw careful to add the compassionate caveat, "I would never sacrifice my children for my political career."

He admitted he has lived a privileged life but said he understood the struggle of many *Sun* readers to make ends meet.

"I have experienced what it is like, setting out on a very modest salary of £10,000 when I started out in London in 1988 and having to pay the rent on a very tight budget," he said. "I can't pretend I had a tough life. But I don't think many MPs have as much experience as I do of failing public services. I have spent night after night sleeping on the floor of Ivan's hospital room and having a shower wherever you can. It's only when you are on a hospital waiting list and you can't have a test you desperately need for six months that you really understand how painful it can be."

After his experiments with drugs and his time in the Bullingdon Club, were there any more skeletons left in his cupboard, he was asked.

"As far as I am concerned, the *Sun* can put a reporter in my bedroom or around my dining room table and come and see the life that I live and he will see a happy and fulfilled and lovely life," he said.

As the contest hotted up, Cameron and Davis went toe to toe on *Question Time* and Davis got the better of him. A poll then put Davis ahead, with fifty per cent of the Tory Party members to Cameron's thirty-seven per cent. But Liam Fox then endorsed Cameron, evening the field.

There was one final ordeal to endure – another interview with Jeremy Paxman, who had creamed Davis the week before. But Cameron had worked in television and knew that image was all in that medium. So he rang the BBC and insisted that he bring his own lights and make-up artist.

"I did not want to look like David Davis did," he said.

Paxman began by asking if Cameron knew what a "pink pussy" was, deliberately to wrong foot him. Cameron's first thought was that it was a nightclub on Ibiza and took comfort in knowing that he had never been there. Next he was asked about a "slippery nipple". He knew this was a drink. It turned out that these were cocktails sold in jugs in the Tiger Tiger chain of bars owned by Urbium, a company whose board Cameron had only recently resigned from. By implication, Cameron was to blame for under-age binge drinking.

The next topic was tuition fees. But Cameron had prepared a nifty counter-attack.

"This is the trouble with these interviews, Jeremy," Cameron said. "You come in, you sit someone down and you treat them like they are some sort of a cross between a fake and a hypocrite and you give them no time to answer their questions."

Later, when he had been interrupted again, he said: "Jeremy, this is farcical. Why don't we have an agreement? Give me two sentences and then you can interrupt."

Seldom had Paxman been so deftly put in his place.

When the result of the ballot of the membership was announced, Cameron had over twice as many votes as Davis with 134,446 to 64,398.

In his acceptance speech at the Royal Academy, he spoke again of the need to build a "modern compassionate Conservative Party", ending: "If you want me and all of us to be a voice for hope, for optimism and for change, come and join us. In this modern, compassionate Conservative Party, everyone is invited."

Afterwards, David, Samantha and Steve Hilton were driven home in the official car of the Leader of the Opposition.

Chapter Nine – Leader of the Opposition

In his leadership acceptance speech, Cameron was seen to have taken a swing at Thatcherism. Now it was time to meet the lady herself. Told it was going to be a "casual" encounter, Cameron wore a jacket and a crisp, white, open-necked shirt. When he was ushered in, the Baroness, then in her eighties, asked which seat he was hoping to stand for at the next election. When informed of her error, Lady Thatcher expressed disbelief that anyone who did not wear a tie could be leader of the Conservative Party.

Those who had supported his leadership bid were given jobs in his inner office and the shadow cabinet, though opponents were also given a fair shake. David Davis was retained as Shadow Home Secretary and George Osborne as Shadow Chancellor. Liam Fox was made Shadow Defence Secretary, but replaced as Shadow Foreign Secretary by William Hague, who had backed Cameron from the beginning. Hague was asked to restore relations with American Republicans. Ed Llewelyn, who Cameron had known since Eton, became his chief of staff and another Conservative research department alumnus, Catherine Fall, became his secretary.

Boris Johnson, who had entered the House alongside Cameron in 2001 and had backed Cameron for the leadership, was relegated to the position of Shadow Minister for Higher Education. Seen as a dangerous rival, he would remain in that post in a subsequent reshuffle.

Determined not to emulate the split between Blair and Brown, Cameron and Osborne shared a suite of offices in the south block of the Norman Shaw Buildings, formerly New Scotland Yard, and had a meeting at 3.30 every afternoon, along with other members of Tory high command.

"They don't just work together. They eat together and holiday together," Tim Montgomerie of the website ConservativeHome said. "This is a huge operation. Cameron is surrounded by people he has known for years, which inspires loyalty and friendship, over necessarily hiring the very best people. It is a close-knit circle."

In his first House of Commons confrontation with Tony Blair, Cameron delighted his supporters, by saying of the Prime Minister: "He was the future once."

Samantha looked on from the public gallery while the press began calling Cameron the "heir to Blair", a phrase crafted by George Osborne. This was not an unmixed blessing. *Private Eye* announced that this was "the world's first face transplant" and Blair accused Cameron of "political cross-dressing".

Cameron had promised to end the Punch and Judy politics of PMQs and back the government when they were right. His first act was to support Blair's loosening of council control over schools which had prompted a rebellion among Labour's left-wing backbenchers.

"With our support, the Prime Minister knows there is no danger of losing these reforms in a parliamentary vote, so he can afford to be as bold as he wants to be," Cameron said.

In an effort to forge a fresh political identity, Cameron embraced the environment and climate change. He was pictured with a dog-sled in the Arctic Circle and got back on his bike. In the local elections, the Conservatives adopted the slogan "Vote Blue Go Green". But the wheels came off when his official chauffeur, Terry, was pictured driving behind his bicycling boss, carrying his shoes in the car.

Cameron admitted that it was a mistake.

"It happened two or three times," he said. "I now have panniers."

He tried to get local Conservative Associations to select more women and non-white candidates, with little success, and his idea to have an A-list favouring women and ethnic minorities had to be dropped. Nevertheless, the Conservatives moved ahead of Labour in the polls and Cameron used his popularity to demand that candidate shortlists should be at least fifty per cent female. Meanwhile, he identified the issues of the country's "obesity crisis" and Britain's "broken society". Though he denied ever saying "hug a hoodie", the headline stuck.

Seeking to give the party a new sense of direction, he published a mini-manifesto called *Built to Last* ahead of the spring conference. A "beefed up" version was re-launched that August, allowing the opposition to call it *Built to Last a Bit Longer*. The party was invited to vote on it. Less than a quarter did so. While 92.7 per cent of those who voted endorsed the document, compared to 7.3 per cent again, only 26.7 per cent of the 247,394 eligible actually voted in the postal ballot.

Cameron put a brave face on it.

"Today's result confirms that the party has changed," he said. "It shows that Conservatives support the vital changes that we have made over the last nine months... over 60,000 people voted. On anyone's account that is a big exercise in party democracy and an overwhelming vote."

Labour chair Hazel Blears called it a "humiliation" for Cameron. When Tony Blair had undertaken a similar exercise with his policy document *New Labour, New Life*, he had a 61 per cent turnout of Labour's 230,000 constituency party members.

At the party conference in October, Cameron wanted to establish his credentials on the NHS. He told the delegates: "When your family relies on the NHS all the time – day after day, night after night – you really know just how precious it is... For me, it's not a question of saying the NHS is 'safe in my hands'. My family is so often in the hands of the NHS. And I want them to be safe there... We will always support the NHS with the funding it needs."

Class reared its ugly head again in a row about grammar schools, known as "grammargate". This gave the newspapers the opportunity to point out that almost everyone in the shadow cabinet was a public-school boy and Cameron's closest advisors were Old Etonians. This was re-enforced by the publication of Elliott and Hanning's *Cameron: The Rise of the New Conservative* which carried a picture of the members of the Bullingdon Club striking ostentatiously arrogant poses. After that, the use of the photograph has been denied by the copyright holders.

Cameron still had no press secretary. What he needed was an attack dog, the equivalent of Blair's Alastair Campbell. He put feelers out, but among his aristocratic cronies there was no one with tabloid experience. However, George Osborne had already had an encounter with Andy Coulson, when the *News of the World* ran claims from former prostitute Natalie Rowe that Osborne had taken cocaine in his early twenties, before he was an MP. Osborne owed Coulson a favour for deliberately down-playing the scandal in the leader column, a lawyer representing phone-hacking victims said.

In January 2007, Coulson had resigned as editor of the *News of the World* over the first phone-hacking scandal which landed royal correspondent Clive Goodman and private investigator Glenn Mulcaire in jail. In March, Osborne suggested to Cameron that Coulson might be the man for the job. The fact that he was a high school boy from Basildon with no whiff of boarding school was another obvious plus.

At the time, Cameron was planning to give the BBC's Guto Harri the position of press secretary, but Rebekah Brooks, then the editor of the *Sun*, suggested the job should go to Coulson to strengthen links between the Conservative Party and News International. The line was, apparently: "If you find something for Andy we will return the favour."

Once Cameron had satisfied himself that Coulson had not known about the phone hacking, he was taken on.

The Conservatives then launched "Stand Up, Speak Up – The Nation's Despatch Box". It was supposed to have been like Labour's "Big Conversation" in 2003, but more interactive. Cameron asked local associations to organize meetings to discuss policy, while the party's website was to host online discussions moderated by the policy group teams. Unfortunately, with six policy groups in action already, the party had more than enough policy initiatives. The whole thing cost £250,000 and the results were a shambles.

"David Cameron yesterday compared reconstructing the Conservative party to building a house," said a leader in the *Guardian*, "and if the metaphor is correct then he must now be staring at heaps of rubble, cement and copper piping, hoping that the architect's plans come together before the first tenants move in."

The suggestion that the Tories would re-introduce entrance fees at museums and art galleries prompted another row about class, as it seemed to suggest that these facilities should be the preserve of a moneyed elite. It had come from shadow Culture Secretary Hugo Swire, an Old Etonian and early Cameron supporter. He was sacked. In the reshuffle, Cameron brought in Sayeeda Warsi as Shadow Minister of State for Community and Social Action. She had to be elevated to the House of Lords as he could not wait for a Muslim woman to be selected as a candidate in a winnable seat.

On the day, Tony Blair stood down, Cameron praised his "considerable achievements... whether it is peace in Northern

Ireland, whether it is his work in the developing world, which I know will endure".

Blair returned the compliment, thanking Cameron for his "generous sentiments" and saying: "I have always found him both proper, direct and courteous in his dealings with me and I thank him for that. And although of course I cannot wish him well politically, personally I wish both him and his family very well indeed."

Cameron then led his party in a standing ovation. It was clear that Cameron and many in his camp admired Blair for taking a party that had been out of office for eighteen years and making it electable again. By contrast, John Major was a "loser", it was said. However, Blair had already warned Cameron that taking on Gordon Brown the next election would be like "a flyweight versus a heavyweight".

"However much he dances around the ring beforehand he will come in reach of a big clunking fist and, you know what, he'll be out on his feet, carried out of the ring," Blair said, thereby receiving a pat on the back from Gordon Brown.

While he acknowledged that Brown had a "great brain", he said: "We're quite happy Blair's going. He's trying to get out of the shit and can't. Brown thinks he still can, so we have to push his face back in it."

And he borrowed from George Orwell's *1984*, claiming that a Brown government would be " like a boot stamping on a human face – for ever".

With Brown now Prime Minister, Cameron referred to him dismissively as "that strange man in Downing Street". His relations with Brown's right-hand man Ed Balls were even worse. Balls had been a contemporary of Cameron's at Oxford where, unlike Cameron, he had joined the university's Conservative Associations – though, he said, only to keep an eye on the enemy. He also got a first in PPE, ahead of Cameron's.

As Brown moved into Number Ten, Quentin Davies, a Tory MP for twenty years, defected to Labour. In his resignation letter, he told Cameron: "Under your leadership the Conservative Party appears to me to have ceased collectively to believe in anything, or to stand for anything. It has no bedrock. It exists on shifting sands. A sense of mission has been replaced by a PR agenda."

The attack was personal. The letter went on: "Although you have many positive qualities, you have three, superficiality, unreliability and an apparent lack of any clear convictions, which in my view ought to exclude you from the position of national leadership."

Cameron said he was not surprised by Davies's decision to cross the floor.

"Thank you for your support in the past," he said dismissively. "We will watch your future career with interest."

Davies became Minister of State for Defence Equipment and Support under Brown and was made a life peer in the 2010 dissolution honours list.

Worse news came when Cameron's handpicked candidate Tony Lit came third in the Ealing Southall by-election, even though Cameron threw everything into the campaign. He was seen personally to blame.

"Slick communication skills may have been enough to put him on the map a year ago," said the *Sunday Times*, "but the electorate has moved on."

More bad luck followed. Cameron had booked a trip to Rwanda when there was an unexpected flood in his Witney constituency and there was talk of a vote of no confidence. Instead of being seen as the Tony Blair of the Conservative Party, Cameron was now seen as its Neil Kinnock.

But Brown failed to capitalize on his opponent's distress and call a snap election. A couple of shocking murders then allowed Cameron to turn the debate to the issue of crime – traditional Tory stamping ground. Failing to call a snap election made Brown appear a ditherer and slowly Cameron's poll ratings revived.

With Brown's ratings now in the doldrums, it seemed likely that he would cling to power for the full five years. This gave the Tories plenty of time to plan, and now Cameron was getting the better of Brown in PMQs.

Then came the credit crunch which dented Brown's reputation for financial competence, which had been the foundation of the whole New Labour project. Then Boris Johnson beat Ken Livingstone to become London's mayor – showing that the Conservatives were electable. Cameron had not picked Boris for the post, regarding his old chum as a loose cannon. But at the victory party, he held Boris's hand aloft as the winner. Cameron later quipped that Boris would not let go – it was "like the first gay marriage". However, he still had to put up with Boris continually sniping at him from his weekly column in the *Daily Telegraph*.

"I sometimes think there are people in politics who ought to be in journalism and there are people in journalism who should be in politics," said Cameron, "but I'm certainly not going to say who."

There was no doubt in anyone's mind who he met.

The Tories had also done well in the local elections outside London, winning forty per cent of the vote against Labour's twenty-seven. Then the Conservatives won a by-election in Crewe and Nantwich, traditionally a solid Labour seat.

Barack Obama's election in 2008 also augured well for Cameron. Change was in the air. On a visit to Britain, Obama was persuaded to visit Cameron's office – though Cameron had introduced the Republican contender John McCain at the 2006 Conservative Party conference. Cameron could now claim to be a player on the world stage and made a play of foreign photo-calls.

He then tried to woo Rupert Murdoch, visiting him on his yacht and attending his daughter Elisabeth's fortieth birthday party on Corfu with George Osborne. It was hosted by the Rothschilds and Osborne seized the opportunity to visit the superyacht of Oleg Deripaska to solicit a donation. This came out because Peter Mandelson had done the same. However, it reminded the public, once again, that Cameron and Osborne moved in wealthy circles. Tiresomely, class was back on the agenda.

The collapse of Lehman Brothers and the resulting financial turmoil allowed Cameron to attack Brown again on the question of financial competence, drawing attention to the spiralling national debt. Brown and Chancellor Alistair Darling "didn't fix the roof when the sun was shining," he said. They had "left Britain running on empty".

There was a brief respite from the political fray when six-year-old Ivan Cameron died. Gordon Brown was sympathetic. He had lost a prematurely born daughter and his second son had been diagnosed with cystic fibrosis, and he cancelled PMQs as a mark of respect. Every child was "precious and irreplaceable", he said, and that the death of a child "was something that no parent should have to bear".

The country was now plunging into recession. But Britain was chair of the G20 and Brown called a summit in London. Deals brokered there saved the world from financial collapse. But Brown's benefit from this achievement was short-lived when his head of communications Damian McBride was caught smearing senior Tories.

When the MPs expenses row broke in 2009, Cameron came out cleaner than most. Although he claimed the maximum for his mortgage on his constituency home, he only had to pay back £680 he had claimed for clearing wisteria and vines from a chimney, replacing outside lights and resealing his conservatory's roof. He apologized for the excesses of his colleagues and warned that those who did not pay back what they owed would be booted out of the party.

With the economy going from bad to worse, Labour would have to make cuts to balance the books, ushering in an age of austerity. This allowed Cameron to ask: "Who made the poorest poorer? Who left youth unemployment higher? Who made inequality greater? No, not the wicked Tories – you, Labour, did this to our society."

At the beginning of 2010, the year of the election, the Conservatives had a double-digit lead in the polls. They should have been shooting at an open goal, but when the momentum seemed to falter Cameron's vacillation over policy was blamed.

By the eve of the spring party conference, the poll lead had closed to just two points. It was then revealed that Conservative donor and deputy party chairman, multi-millionaire Lord Ashcroft, was a "non-dom", avoiding paying UK tax on his earnings outside Britain. This was just the sort of image the Cameron wanted to leave behind.

Once the election was called on 6 April, Cameron travelled to contested seats in Yorkshire and the West Midlands, reinforcing a classless image by addressing party workers in an open-necked shirt with his sleeves rolled up.

Cameron had long advocated TV debates, knowing that Brown was a poor performer on the box.

"I've been calling for these debates for five years," he said. "I challenged Blair, I challenged Brown, I challenged when I was ahead in the polls, and when I was behind in the polls. I just think they are a good thing."

However, it was Nick Clegg who benefited from the TV exposure in the first round and Cameron, understandably, was less enthusiastic about the next two. With over two weeks and one TV debate to go, Cameron already knew he was in trouble. Close advisors gathered at his house with a copy of the Lib Dem manifesto and their own to begin roughing out a draft coalition agreement. In public, though, they were still warning of the dire consequences of a hung parliament.

On the campaign trail, Cameron made light of the fact that he was being followed by a man dressed as a chicken – a stunt by the Labour-supporting *Daily Mirror* – by pulling off the bird's head. When he was hit by an egg the next day in Cornwall, he got the opportunity to quip, deadpan: "Now I know what came first: it was the chicken not the egg."

With the TV debates at an end, the wind came out of the Lib Dems' sails and Brown made a gaff. Accidentally leaving his radio mike on, he referred to a Rochdale pensioner as a "bigoted woman". Brown had to make a grovelling apology.

Cameron and Osborne spent polling day at Steve Hilton's farmhouse near Dean. Each gave their forecast for the final tally of seats. They knew they had not made it.

Chapter Ten – The Premiership

After the count in Witney, David Cameron was driven back to Conservative HQ, now in Millbank Tower. He was greeted by the party donors who made it clear that he had let them down. Ashcroft had already given an interview blaming the TV debates for robbing the Conservatives of a majority. Cameron knew how ruthless the party could be and faced the very real possibility of being chucked out on his ear.

The object now was to make a coalition with the Lib Dems. The only other possibility was to form a minority government. But this would risk another election within a few months when, Cameron thought, they were unlikely to do any better. By then, the party might even consider running under another leader. However, he could claim some success – he had gained more seats in a single election than Mrs Thatcher ever had and had made the largest gain for his party since 1931. A Con-Dem coalition was the only way ahead. He would brook no opposition.

Gordon Brown appeared on television saying he would remain as Prime Minister while the Conservatives and Liberal Democrats held talks. If their talks came to nothing, he would explore the possibility of a Lib-Lab pact, which would offer "electoral reform" – the proportional representation that the Lib Dems had long sought.

Clearly as the Conservatives had 306 seats – against Labour's 258 and the Lib Dem's 57 – they should take the first turn in trying to form a government. Cameron told the press: "I want to make a big, open and comprehensive offer to the Liberal Democrats. I want us to work together in tackling our country's big and urgent problems – the debt crisis, our deep social problems and our broken political system."

While two teams of top advisors had a series of meetings to thrash out the details, Cameron and Clegg discussed the matter privately. Clegg was insistent on one thing – electoral reform.

Talks had to be broken off on 8 May for a ceremony at the Cenotaph, marking the sixty-fifth anniversary of VE Day. The three party leaders stood shoulder to shoulder in Whitehall. The negotiations resumed the following day.

Clegg and Brown also held talks. There were conflicting accounts of how they went. The Lib Dems were insistent that Gordon Brown would have to stand down as Prime Minister immediately if there was to be a pact. He announced that he would only step down in September after the Labour Party had elected a new leader. Another stumbling block was that even a coalition between Labour and the Liberal Democrats would not give them the 326 seats they needed for an outright majority. Other parties would have to be brought on board.

The Conservatives offered the Lib Dems a referendum on the Alternative Vote, their preferred system of proportional representation. Labour then promised to introduce AV with a referendum afterwards to approve it. Meanwhile, Labour tried to persuade the SNP and other smaller parties to join a rainbow coalition.

When that failed, Brown went to Buckingham Palace to tender his resignation. Cameron became Prime Minister an hour later, though the coalition agreement had not yet been finalized. Arriving at Number Ten with Samantha, he announced his determination to form a coalition government, rather than govern with a minority administration.

At 10pm, Cameron was greeted with cheers by Conservative MPs in the Committee Room of the House of Commons. Shortly after midnight on 12 May – six days after the election – the Lib Dems approved the coalition agreement, which was published later that day. That afternoon, Cameron and his new Deputy Prime Minister Nick Clegg held a press conference in Downing Street's Rose Garden. Their legislative programme was outlined at the State Opening of Parliament on 25 May and Cameron faced his first PMQs as Prime Minister on 2 June.

Asked why he wanted to be Prime Minister, he said: "Because I thought I would be good at it."

Few predicted that the coalition would hang together for the full five years. It has not been an easy ride. George Osborne's austerity policies to cut the deficit were bound to be unpopular with those affected by government cutbacks, pay freezes and benefits cuts.

David Cameron also found himself mired in the phone-hacking scandal. He had brought Andy Coulson with him to Downing Street as director of communications. It was then discovered that he was still being paid by News International after he had been hired by Cameron.

In 2013, he appeared in the dock of the Old Bailey alongside Rebekah Brooks and others, charged with phone hacking offences. He was found guilty on one charge of conspiracy to hack phones.

While the jury was still considering its verdict, Cameron issued a statement saying: "I take full responsibility for employing Andy Coulson. I did so on the basis of undertakings I was given by him about phone hacking and those turned out not to be the case. I always said that if they turned out to be wrong, I would make a full and frank apology and I do that today. I am extremely sorry that I employed him. It was the wrong decision and I am very clear about that."

This drew a rebuke from the judge for commenting on Coulson's guilt before the trial had ended. He was sentenced to eighteen months in prison. He also faced a trial for perjury in Scotland.

Brooks was cleared of all charges, but she was forced to resigned from her position as chief executive of News International after the closure of the *News of the World*. During the scandal it was revealed that she was a close friend of neighbour David Cameron, who used to ride horses on her Oxfordshire farm. They also socialized with Rupert Murdoch's son James. His sister, Elisabeth, is another member of the so-called Chipping Norton set, along with Jeremy Clarkson. Cameron dressed up as The Stig for Clarkson's fiftieth birthday party. It also came out that Coulson had been Brooks' lover.

Under Cameron, British support for rebels in Libya helped bring down Colonel Gaddafi. As the Arab Spring spread, his government sought to support the rebels in Syria after the use of chemical weapons by forces commanded by Bashar al-Assad, but Cameron lost the vote in the House of Commons. This was the first time a British government had been blocked from taking military action by parliament.

"I strongly believe in the need for a tough response to the use of chemical weapons but I also believe in respecting the will of this House of Commons," Cameron said. "It is clear to me that the British parliament, reflecting the views of the British people, does not want to see British military action. I get that and the Government will act accordingly."

Congress followed suit, preventing President Obama from taking any military action. This has allowed the Islamic State to flourish there and left NATO looking impotent in the face to Russian aggression in the Ukraine.

Victory in by the Scottish National Party in the 2011 Scottish general election forced Cameron's government to concede a referendum on independence. As the vote neared, an opinion poll put the "yes" campaign ahead. This caused panic as Cameron feared that he might be remembered as the Prime Minister who oversaw the break-up of the United Kingdom. Gordon Brown rode to the rescue and, with just two days to go, the three main UK parties pledged to devolve extensive new powers to the Scottish parliament if the "no" vote won.

In the end the Scottish people did vote "no".

"I am delighted," said Cameron. "It would have broken my heart to see our United Kingdom come to an end and I know that this sentiment was shared not just by people across our country, but also around the world."

He also faced problems with the European Union, who asked for more than £1.7 billion in budget payments. Cameron refused to pay. George Osborne later claimed victory on the dispute, noting that the UK would not have to pay additional interest on the payments, which would be delayed until after Britain's general election on 7 May 2015.

As that election approached Cameron put strict provisos on the TV debates, fearing they would hurt him again as they had in 2010. He would prefer to fight the election on signs that the economy was reviving.

Clearly, this time, class will not be an issue. While Ed Miliband was the son of immigrant parents, his father went on to have a distinguished academic career. Ed and his brother David attended the same primary school as Boris Johnson in Primrose Hill. Although Ed went to a comprehensive school, like Cameron, he worked as an intern for an MP and family friend, in his case Tony Benn. He, too, read PPE at Oxford. Asked about his "life experience" outside politics, he replied that he had lectured at Harvard and had been a special advisor to Gordon Brown at the Treasury.

Nick Clegg was the son of the chairman of United Trust Bank and was descended from Russian nobility. He was a public school boy, having been to Westminster School, and went on to Cambridge, the University of Minnesota and the College of Europe in Bruges. His wife was the daughter of a Spanish senator. Outside politics, he has been a ski instructor and a journalist. Otherwise, he has worked as a lobbyist and for the European Commission. He is, however, passionate about social mobility. Under the coalition, he set up the Social Mobility Commission under Alan Milburn.

There was, of course, one would-be "man of the people" in the 2015 election – Nigel Farage, the leader of UKIP. His father was a stockbroker. Another public school boy, he went to Dulwich College. He made his money as a commodity broker in the City.

But as Cameron often declares: "It doesn't matter where you come from. It's where you are going that counts."

Certainly, Cameron is going into the history books, which will not judge him on his social class. They will simply have to decide whether he is a class act.

Blond Ambition

The Rise and Rise of Boris Johnson

Chapter One – The Birth of the Blond

Before the 2015 election, Boris Johnson wrote *The Churchill Factor*, a biography of Britain's wartime leader, inviting comparisons with the great man himself. Both had trans-Atlantic connections. Churchill's mother was Brooklyn beauty Jennie Jerome. Boris was born in New York, in a low-rent hospital on the Upper East Side of Manhattan. His parents were in the States on his father Stanley's Harkness Fellowship, which funds UK students' studies in America. Stanley Johnson was determined to secure joint citizenship for his son and registered his birth with both the US authorities and the British consulate. So, technically, Boris is eligible to become President of the United States.

His parents had met when they were students at Oxford. Stanley had won the prestigious Newdigate Prize for poetry, once won by Oscar Wilde. Daughter of the bursar of All Soul's, Sir James Fawcett, Charlotte attended the ceremony where Stanley read an extract from his winning entry. They had tea in her halls soon after and married the following spring.

While Stanley had been a staunch Conservative since school, Charlotte came from a long line of liberal lefties, which included leading lights from the Suffragettes and a radical MP who sat in Gladstone's Liberal administration in 1880. Her parents were close friends with campaigners Lord and Lady Longford. Charlotte's mother was a Catholic convert of Jewish extraction. Charlotte herself had been on CND and anti-apartheid rallies, while her brother has worked for the New Left Books before adding a little radical zest to the *Economist*.

Stanley took a course in creative writing – then in its infancy – at the State University of Iowa. Then they returned to New York, where Stanley enrolled on an economics course at Columbia University. They lived in a loft on West 23rd Street, opposite the Chelsea Hotel where Dylan Thomas was staying when he died.

As a condition of the scholarship, Stanley had to travel widely. So in May 1964, when Charlotte was eight months pregnant, they drove down to Texas. Unable to take the car out of the country, they travelled on to Mexico City by Greyhound bus. There they met up with Boris Litwin, a Russian émigré whose daughter Stanley had known at Oxford.

Litwin was appalled that Stanley intended to take the heavily pregnant Charlotte back to New York the way they had come and bought them airline tickets so they could fly back. In gratitude, Charlotte said she would name the baby Boris, whichever sex it turned out to be.

Stanley could not be persuaded to attend more than one of his wife's antenatal clinics and, at the moment of birth, he had popped out for a pizza. The child was born on 19 June 1964 a robust 9lb 1oz and already, at birth, had a disordered mop of platinum blonde hair.

The origin of this is supposed to have been the blond-haired inhabitants of the Turkish village of Kalfat in north-west Anatolia, where Boris's great-great-grandfather had come from. His mother was said to have been a blue-eyed Circassian slave girl.

Boris's great-grandfather, Ali Kemal, was an Anglophile Turkish politician who fell foul of the Nationalists in 1922, during the birth pangs of the Turkish Republic. His first wife who was a half-English, half-Swiss woman had given birth to their son, Osman Ali. She died in childbirth and the boy was brought up by Margaret Johnson in Southbourne-on-Sea, Dorset. Osman Ali became Wilfred Johnson. His son, Stanley, would be another blond.

Boris himself would be christened Alexander Boris de Pfeffel Johnson. In the family, Boris was always known as Al and his first article in *The Times* appears under the by-line Alexander Johnson. The "de Pfeffel" comes from his grandmother, Irène, wife of Wilfred "Johnny" Johnson, who was born in the Versailles home of Baron de Pfeffel. According to BBC's *Who Do You Think You Are?*, Irène was the granddaughter of an actress and Prince Paul von Wüttenberg, a descendant of George II, making Boris an eighth cousin to David Cameron. Granny Butter, as Boris knew her, maintained her aristocratic pretensions to the end and urged Stanley to look into the possibility of claiming a French barony.

Soon after Boris was born, his parents decided to return to England so that Charlotte could complete her English degree. But first, they made a tour of New England and Canada. Throughout it all, Boris was said to have been an unbelievably good baby.

Back in Oxford, Boris amused himself while his mother, already seven months pregnant with her second child, prepared for her finals. It was later discovered that he was so quiet and self-contained because he was deaf. The condition, "glue ear", regularly confined him to bed as a child. At the age of eight or nine, the problem was solved when he underwent a series of operations to put grommets in his ears. But his early deafness left him with a curious detachment and a great capacity for reading.

In July 1965, the family moved to Crouch End in north London. After teaching, studying for a Masters in Agricultural Economics and, according to his own account, being recruited as a spy, Stanley was offered a job at the World Bank in Washington DC. But first the family moved to a rented cottage on Exmoor where Stanley wrote his first novel *Gold Drain*.

Moving to Washington in February 1966, they lived for a month in the Dupont Plaza Hotel, before moving into a clapboard house in the northwest of the city. Boris's first memory is of playing in the tree-house in the garden there.

The children were looked after by a series of au pairs, none of whom stayed long, while their parents moved in distinguished circles that included the veteran BBC correspondent Charles Wheeler.

In 1968, as an April Fool's Day joke, Stanley applied for a $100-million loan to finance the building of three more pyramids to boost Egypt's tourist trade. The new president of the World Bank, former Secretary of Defense Robert McNamara, did not see the funny side and Stanley was fired. He got a new job with the Population Council, set up by John D. Rockefeller III in New York. The family lived a house in Connecticut. As part of his work, Stanley travelled a great deal and there were more short-lived au pairs.

There were riots in the US in 1968 and Charlotte wanted to return to England. They flew home the following year and moved to Nethercote in the Exmoor river valley, where Stanley's parents had a farmhouse. His sister also lived there briefly and Stanley's family moved into the family compound. Conditions were primitive.

Stanley loved the place, though he was sent away to boarding school at Sherborne, which he also lauded in his autobiography *Stanley I Presume*. Though poor, his family, he thought, had breeding and a certain class. He claimed never to have met a grammar school boy until he went up to Oxford on scholarship at the age of nineteen. This sense of superiority gave him an arrogance that led him to think it was all right to break the rules as long as you did so in style.

Though Boris resembled his father in many ways, it was said that his intelligence came from his mother. She read to the children and made sure that their interests were literary and highbrow. They were taught to value education and ambition. Boris's own competitive edge was honed when his sister Rachel, just fifteen months younger than him, learnt to read first. As a child he was not content to grow up to be Prime Minister or President, he said he wanted to be "world king".

Cheering him on was Stanley, who flew into a rage if Boris did not outdo his siblings. Coming second would never do, said Stanley, it was emphatically *not* about taking part.

Dinner guests at Nethercote were treated to the spectacle of Stanley and Boris sparring like alpha males, with the younger children finding it hard to get a word in. On one occasion, Boris came to blows with Rachel over the name of the lead singer of The Clash. On another, younger brother Leo shot Boris with an air gun. Though he was rushed to hospital for emergency treatment the incident was treated as a joke in the Johnson household. Nevertheless, the family were close and, after moving frequently as a child and now cut off in a remote farmhouse, Boris found it difficult to make friends outside the family.

In 1969, Stanley got a grant from the Ford Foundation to do post-graduate research at the London School of Economics and the family moved to a house in Maida Vale, rented from a friend of Charlotte's parents. Taking time off from study, he joined the Conservative Research Department where he met up-and-coming Tory grandees Douglas Hurd and Chris Patten.

When Stanley headed off around the world researching another book, the family went back to Nethercote, where Boris went to Winsford Village School. After Stanley returned, they bought a home in Primrose Hill, London NW1, and Boris attended Primrose Hill Primary School, later the alma mater of both David and Ed Miliband. Thanks to a windfall – Stanley complained that he had always been dogged by good luck – the family moved into a larger house nearby to accommodate the brood that had now swelled to four.

Their next move was to Brussels, where Stanley exercised his environmental concerns as head of the Prevention of Pollution and Nuisance Division of the European Commission. At the European School in the outlying suburb of Uccle, Boris met a girl named Marina Wheeler, daughter of Charles Wheeler and his Sikh wife Dip. She had just arrived from Washington and impressed Boris with her "Impeach Nixon" badge. On the other hand, she decided he was "generally to be avoided" and the Johnsons were "wild and out of control".

At the European school, Boris was identified as a gifted child. But at home things were going badly wrong. Charlotte was having a nervous breakdown. Suffering from depression, she spent nine months in the Maudsley Hospital in London, where Boris and the other children would visit her. After that, she was in and out of hospital quite often and, even when she was at home, she did not seem entirely well.

Boris and Rachel took over the role of child care of their younger siblings. Rachel was cast as Wendy to Boris's Peter Pan, with their two younger brothers, Jo and Leo, playing the Lost Boys.

Chapter Two – Boarders

In September 1975, eleven-year-old Boris and Rachel, then ten, were packed off to Ashdown House, a prep school in Sussex. The children would make the trip there themselves. Before the era of Eurostar, they would be dropped at the Gare du Nord in Brussels with a packed lunch and take the train to Ostend. They would take the ferry to Dover, then the train to Victoria. After a stop at the Cartoon Cinema – though Boris later favoured the British Museum – they would take the train to East Grinstead. The journey would take the whole day.

Once, returning at the end of term, they managed to get on the train bound for Moscow instead of the one for Brussels. Again, the event was treated as a comedy rather than a potential catastrophe.

Just before Christmas in 1978, Charlotte and Stanley separated. Stanley took the blame. It was his constant philandering that had caused the split. The au pairs were a particular target. Boris recalled how, in the hot summer of 1976, they used to walk around temptingly naked. He later confided that, after his parents had split, he decided to make himself emotionally invulnerable.

Boris's parents divorced when he was fourteen. The family home was sold and Charlotte moved into a flat in Notting Hill, where she became a portrait painter. Sitters included Joanna Lumley and Jilly

Cooper. Though she was short of money, the children often used to stay with her and she found Boris very supportive.

In 1988, she married an American academic and moved to New York, returning a widow in 1996, again living in Notting Hill. By then she was suffering from Parkinson's disease.

Boris found school life at Ashdown House "idyllic", except for one thing – the regular beatings he received from masters. He became a vehement opponent of corporal punishment. It was the one of the few subjects he was said to talk seriously on.

"I remember being so enraged at being whacked for talking at the wrong moment that it has probably given me a lifelong distrust of authority," he wrote in 2009.

At Ashdown House, Boris – already a P.G. Wodehouse fan – began creating his persona of a bumbling English eccentric of 1930s' vintage, though some of it must have been borrowed from his father. He also excelled academically, particularly at Latin and Greek, and won a King's Scholarship to Eton. At sports, he was not so gifted, but he was an enthusiastic rugby player. This lent him a certain physical assurance.

In 1979, Stanley was elected Conservative MEP for Wight and Hampshire East. Soon after, he met Jennifer Kidd, a left-leaning former editor at Weidenfeld & Nicholson. They married in 1981 and she gave him two further children, Julia and Maximilian, both of whom were blonds. This brought with it a new round of sibling rivalry.

Chapter Three – Eton Mess

Having entered Eton as a King's Scholar – even though he had scraped in thirteenth – Boris was one of the intellectual elite and his hair made him instantly recognizable. However, he was not among the social elite, known as the Oppidans, who had got there by dint of money.

After a term mucking in with the Oppidans, Boris was given a room in College, the Scholars' house. Dating from the Middle Ages, it was the oldest building in the school. The regime there was more liberal than the true-blue houses where the fee-paying boys lived. The denizens were known as "Tugs", because of the gowns –"togas" – Scholars must wear at all times. Nevertheless, Boris was quickly inculcated into the school's ethos that Etonians were groomed to be future leaders, duty-bound to repay society for the privileges that had been bestowed on them. Clearly, Old Etonians were destined to rule over others.

Among the Scholars, Boris did not distinguish himself, but he was certainly much brighter than the other boys. His house master David Guilford, who also taught him Classics, called him "an all-rounder, very good at rugby and the Wall Game, but perhaps less at cricket. He was a School figure – unusual for a Scholar."

Guilford also taught David Cameron but remembered nothing of him, though Cameron was considered "posh" by contemporaries, even by the standards of Eton.

Determined to stand out, A.B. – Al or Alex – Johnson slowly became the more distinctive "Boris". Desperate to fit in, he abandoned his mother's Catholicism for the Church of England and, while his new-found poshness was a mere façade, he pulled it off with humour and perfect comic timing.

Boris was perfectly in tune with the times. Michael McCrum had become headmaster in 1970. He favoured academic excellence over social cachet. Fagging and caning were being phased out.

While spotty and swotty, Boris shone during debates, even deflecting difficult questions from masters. His performance in Maths and Science was not good, but he excelled in Classics.

After a shaky start in English, he went on to win the English prize, developing his familiar style in the school magazine, *The Chronicle*. When the former Prime Minister visited the school's Political Society, which Boris later ran, he wrote: "Edward Heath was lit up from behind, his face in the shade and a halo of silver light extending from his temples, like a prophet of old."

Boris's style is notable again in a spirited defence of privilege he wrote in December 1980: "I tell you this. The Civilized World can ignore, must ignore these idiots who tell us that by their very existence public schools demolish all hopes most cherished for the Comprehensive System. Clearly, this is twaddle, utter bunkum, balderdash, tommyrot, piffle and fiddlesicks of the most insidious kind. So strain every nerve, parents of Britain, to send your son to this educational establishment (forget this socialist gibberish about the destruction of the State System). Exercise your freedom of choice because in this way you imbue your son with the most important thing, a sense of his own importance."

Three years later, in an interview with *The Chronicle*, Ken Livingstone, then leader of the soon-to-be-abolished Greater London Council and later Boris's rival for Mayor of London, gave a riposte.

"I think your school," he said, "should be integrated into the state system, because I don't think you have the right [through] what your parents can buy [to] a privileged start over the rest of society. I look at the people who have emerged from Eton and Harrow, Oxford and Cambridge and I think you're a load of bloody wallies."

The young Boris's awards included the Newcastle Classical Prize, though his masters complained about the lateness and presentation of his work. It was said that he lacked a "commitment to the real business of scholarship". A report sent to his father mentioned his "disgracefully cavalier attitude", his "sheer feckless" and "gross failure of responsibility" despite being "surprised at the same time that he was not appointed Captain of the School".

"I think he honestly believes that it is churlish of us not to regard him as exceptional," it went on, "one who should be free of the network obligation which binds us to everyone else."

The author also mentions that he is "enormously fond of Boris" and praises his performance in the College play where he played the comic figure Sir Politique Would-be. There was even talk of him going to Harvard.

Later, the same teacher complained: "Boris is pretty impressive when success can be achieved by pure intelligence unaccompanied by hard work. He is, in fact, pretty idle about it all. Boris has something of an tendency to assume that success and honour will drop into his lap…"

He was even forty-five minutes late for a meeting with the provost. When the provost, naturally, took offence, Boris said it was because he wanted to invite Ronald Reagan to speak at the Political Society.

The report continued: "It was perhaps a bit of a risk to make Boris Captain of the School: but he clearly has the personality and the respect necessary for the job…"

The master later explained that, despite appearances, Boris was not a rebel at all. "He was a fully signed up member of the tribe. He was jolly nearly the custodian of the ark. Everything that went into the traditions of being at College, Boris embraced whole-heartedly – Latin prayers, bellowed hymns."

Boris also came to the fore in the Wall Game, which pitted the Scholars against the Oppidans. While protesting against the Vietnam war conducted by US President Lyndon Baines Johnson, he chanted: "Hey, hey, LBJ, how many kids did you kill today?". *The Chronicle* ran: "Hey, hey, ABJ, how many Oppidans did you kill today?"

It also told spectators to "watch the blond Behemoth crud relentlessly through the steaming pile of purple-and-orange

[Oppidan] heavyweights". His own wild disregard of his safety and that of others when playing rugby was also noted.

Recklessly ambitious, he also became editor of *The Chronicle*, bringing in a coterie that included Andrew Gilmour, son of Sir Ian Gilmour, then Privy Seal in Margaret Thatcher's government; Darius Guppy, later jailed in an insurance swindle; and Viscount Althorp, later Earl Spencer, brother of Princess Diana. At parties at Althorp, Boris rubbed shoulders with genuine toffs, giving a decided leg-up to the first-generation Etonian – Sherborne was not considered top-draw. Boris went on to become a member of "Pop", Eton's self-electing elite. They wore checked, spongebag trousers and waistcoats, and were above the admonitions of masters.

But Boris did not just cultivate aristocrats. He made friends with the few black pupils there were at Eton, who were otherwise ignored. Then there were girls.

As secretary of the Debating Society, he organized trips to girls' schools for competitions. He was already star of the debating team, and some were picking him out as a future PM. One female contestant was particularly impressed as Boris seemed to knock up his speech after arriving at the venue, scribbling it on a piece of paper on the back of a tree.

Boris spoke in favour of the motion "This House would Emigrate" in 1981, when Mrs Thatcher's economic policies had decimated British industry and laid much of the country to waste. On that occasion, he lost the vote.

Boris was rarely a loser, though music was not his forte. Determined to triumph in the piano competition, he set about trying to learn the instrument. Though he struggled manfully, he did not have the co-ordination, failing Grade 1 despite "months of brow-beading effort". Years earlier, he had been bested on the recorder by his sister Rachel. And later, he was ousted from a rock band when he failed to master the opening bars of "Smoke on the Water" on the bass guitar.

A new headmaster took over at Eton in 1980. This was Sir Eric Anderson, who had previously been Tony Blair's housemaster at Fettes. He spotted a similarity between the two boys.

"Both of them opted to live on their wits rather than preparation," he said. "They both enjoyed performing. In both cases people found them life-enhancing and fun to have around, but also maddening."

Famously, when Boris was playing the lead in *Richard III*, he could not be bothered to learn his lines, so he pasted them on the back of various pillars. He spent the performance dashing from pillar to pillar, fluffing his lines and causing much amusement – except to the rest of the cast who had learnt theirs.

Anderson once gave Boris's sixth-form class ten minutes to write down what the words "business, industry and commerce" suggested. Boris's essay was succinct.

"These words suggest to me that the headmaster dined in London last night," he said. He was right. Anderson later said that Boris was the most interesting pupil he had ever had.

"Anyone who's spent an hour with Boris never forgets it," he said.

Whatever his shortcomings, Boris could not have been faulted in Classics and won a scholarship to Balliol College, Oxford – normally considered the home of "lefties", and not the natural habitat of High Tories such as Trinity, Christ Church or Magdalen, where his mates Althorp and Guppy went.

On his page on Eton's College Leaving Book, Boris put a picture of himself toting a machine gun and note of his ambition to put "more notches on my phallocratic phallus". In fact, he saw Oxford as the place he would find the pick of potential wives. Once married, he thought, he could get on with the serious business of his career.

Chapter Four – Bullingdon and Beyond

Boris spent his gap year teaching English and Latin at Geelong Grammar School – Australia's Eton – at the Timbertop campus where Prince Charles had spent two terms. A sojourn digging latrines for starving children in Africa was not for Boris.

It is unclear whether Boris dabbled in drugs around this time. On occasions, he has admitted to puffing on the odd joint. Once, on *Have I Got News for You*, he said he had even been offered cocaine – "but I sneezed and so it did not go up my nose. In fact, I may have been doing icing sugar". Since Bill Clinton's admission that he had once smoked a joint but "did not inhale", it has been important for politicians not to seem completely out of touch, while not alienating Middle England – or, indeed, Middle America.

When Boris arrived at Balliol in the autumn of 1983, Oxford was still basking in the reflected glory of the TV series of *Brideshead Revisited*, which had its own blond hero, Lord Sebastian Flyte, played by Anthony Andrews. It was packed with other OEs who ran their own "invitation only" clubs. One such was the Bullingdon.

Putatively founded in 1780 as an all-male sporting club, its membership was limited to thirty. Boris, David Cameron and George Osborne were all members, though Boris, with his comparatively modest background, was way down the pecking order.

Over the years, it had become a dining and drinking club and its drunken antics were legendary. Once, when a pot plant was thrown through a restaurant window, Boris claimed to have joined the others overnight in a police cell. No charges were pressed. Some doubt whether he was actually there. But it seems that he signed up to this Bertie-Woosterish prank anyway – though at the *Telegraph* Max Hastings compared him to newt-fancier Gussie Fink-Nottle.

Others note that Boris does not like to be out of control, either on drink or drugs. Nor, like his fellow members, could he afford to pick up the tab for the damage done. It was the Bullingdon way to trash the place, then buy their way out of the consequence. Boris did not have that sort of cash behind him.

What he did need, though, was for the other Old Etonians to stand behind him. Though the university had made some efforts to be more egalitarian during the 1960s, it was still home to toffs. They looked down on anyone who was not from the three top-line public schools – Eton, Harrow and Winchester – again as "Tugs". Those from grammar schools were "Stains". Beyond that, alumni of comprehensive schools were simply beyond the pale.

Boris expected other OEs to gather round when he made his first bid for power. However, he turned up half-an-hour too late to put his name down for a position on the Treasurer's Committee of the Oxford Union. This did not stop him running for the prestigious position of secretary the following summer. The OEs won it for him. This gave him a platform to run for president of the Union, which, in earlier times, was seen as a sure stepping stone to the top in politics.

Standing against him was a grammar-school boy Neil Sherlock – a Stain. But Boris had a secret weapon. He had bagged a prestigious girlfriend, Allegra Mostyn-Owen. She was the daughter of Christie's chairman Willie Mostyn-Owen, OE – a descendent of Owen Glendower, the last Welsh prince of Wales – and his socialite wife Gaia. They had a stately home, Woodhouse, in Shropshire and a seventeenth-century castle Perthshire – Gaia once admitted she had no idea of how many rooms it had.

Not only was Allegra fiercely intelligent – studying Politics, Philosophy and Economics at Trinity – she was a sought-after beauty. Terence Donovan photographed her for *Vogue* and David Bailey got her on the cover of *Tatler*. Boris won her with his typical style. Hearing that she was having a party, he turned up a night early with a bottle of wine, saying he had mistaken the date. She did not know him, but she had been reading a dusty book on economics and invited him in. They drank the bottle of wine and chatted. He made her laugh. They became friends. Then he indicated that, unless they became an item, he would have to spend more time on his work at the Union. He was soon the envy of every heterosexual man at the university and this prize raised his social standing considerably.

Allegra also had other uses. When Boris was running for the presidency, she invited Neil Sherlock to tea in her rooms and implored him not to impede the progress of her beau. Despite her obvious charms, Sherlock's head was not turned and he smelled a rat when Boris turned up as he was leaving. Plainly, Boris was desperate and traditionally you are not supposed to canvass for votes in Union elections. But while Boris could depend on the support of the OEs, he overstepped the mark handing out free bottles of wine to prominent members of the constituency. This was simply not done. He appeared to be trying too hard and Sherlock won easily.

Boris was shocked. This setback shook his OE sense of entitlement. Even at Oxford, it seemed, a toff could no longer trump trade. For this brief interlude at least, it seemed the class war had been lost.

During the summer vacation of 1985, Boris and Allegra went on a tour of Portugal and Spain with Rachel and her boyfriend Sebastian Shakespeare. To fund their contribution to the trip, Boris and Rachel decided to produce a report on animal cruelty for the World Wildlife Fund, secured through Stanley. They researched bullfighting, the mistreatment of donkeys and the use of monkeys as props by beach photographers.

Allegra's contribution was her contacts. Wherever they went, instead of staying in some grotty B&B, she found a local aristo or oligarch to put them up.

Though Boris was only twenty-one, it was clear he had made his mind up to marry his princess. But he did not pass muster with her family. Her father found him "rapacious" and "wilfully scruffy", while Gaia scared him. When he went skiing with the family, Boris left his passport behind so had to catch a later flight. When he turned up, he found the only thing in his suitcase was his dirty sheets from Balliol. He had to ski in his normal clothes – moleskin trousers and a tweed jacket – like an Edwardian gentleman. He also told Allegra's mother that he could not ski, then impressed her with his daredevil antics.

Allegra and Boris had one thing in common. They were both fiercely competitive.

"They used to compete on everything, even down to who had the best orgasm," a friend said.

It was clear to one and all that Boris and Allegra were, albeit unofficially, engaged. For ever-ambitious Stanley, Allegra was something of a catch. However, he managed to dampen the ardour of Sebastian Shakespeare, and Rachel went on to marry a genuine blue-blood named Ivo Dawnay.

Back at Oxford, Allegra became editor of the student magazine *Isis* with Rachel and Darius Guppy in tow, while Boris threw himself back into student politics. He now realized that, to get elected, he had to broaden his appeal beyond his core OE voters. Steering clear of Guppy, he was now everyone's friend. He learned another lesson. When it came to the business of garnering votes, he must not appear too gritty or thrusting, or too party political. But it was easy for Boris to hide his overweening ambition under a cloak of Johnsonian buffoonery.

Briefly the Social Democratic Party, or SDP, had made an appearance in national politics. Boris let everyone think he was a supporter. He also employed "stooges" – one of whom was Michael Gove – and he co-opted American student Frank Luntz, later a successful pollster in the US, to analyse the electorate. Disregarding Luntz's advice to stick with Reagan-Thatcher conservatism, Boris was determined to be everything to everyone. He was into conciliation rather than Thatcherite confrontation. He even spoke up for proportional representation. Boris won with a thumping majority and the national newspapers began running pieces about the new president of the Oxford Union and his eye-catching girlfriend.

It is generally agreed that Boris did not do much with the Union once he had won the presidency – other than use it as a stepping stone for a future career in journalism. He invited Max Hastings, editor of the *Daily Telegraph*, and Anthony Howard, a family friend and deputy editor of the *Observer*, to speak, while he held sway as from the speaker's chair.

Allegra encouraged this because, to preside at debates, Boris had to turn out in evening dress, rather than his usual shabby attire. However, Union staff kept a bottle of Tippex on hand to paint over the stains that regularly appeared on his shirt-front.

The role of president attracted a certain amount of female attention. Women offered to wash his clothes for him and buy him shampoo – things that Boris was, evidently, too busy to do. To hold on to her man, the aristocratic Allegra had to take on these menial roles.

As president of the Union, Boris got his first taste of power. The Union had a staff of fourteen and a turnover of a quarter of a million pounds. Boris held sway over this empire from the thirty-foot long, book-lined office – which he would hardly match as Mayor of London.

As soon as the term of office was over, Boris abandoned his SDP credentials. The stooges who had helped him were ruthlessly abandoned. At the 1987 general election, he proudly donned the blue rosette again. Some of his contemporaries accused him of having no political beliefs at all. Boris agreed. Apart from "vague sensations of enthusiasm when the Falklands were recaptured," he said, "I did not give a monkey's … I had viewed politics with a perfectly proper mixture of cynicism and apathy. Whatever I read under the bedclothes, it certainly wasn't Hansard."

Then, he recalled being asked to contribute towards the miners, who were on strike. For Boris, it was an epiphany: "… as I reached for my pocket, I found myself remembering some stuff I'd read about these miners, and the chaos they were causing with their illegal strike," he wrote twenty years later. "Oi, I said to my fellow-student. No, I said. I won't give any dosh to these blasted strikers, because, as far as I can see, they are being execrably led, haven't had a proper ballot and are plainly trying to bring down the elected government of the country."

When Stanley Johnson went up to Oxford in the 1960s, he had set himself three goals – to win a Blue at rugby, to become president of the Union and to get a first. He achieved none of these. Likewise, Boris had set himself three goals – to find a wife, to become president of the Union and get a first. He had succeeded in the first two. Now he settled down to work on the third. In earlier terms, Boris had winged it. At tutorials, where students were expected to read out their essays, Boris would appear empty handed and ad lib.

Once his presidency was over, though, he disappeared into the library and set about swotting, but missed a first by a hair's breadth and had to settle for the top 2:1 in his year.

Chapter Five – Boris Goes to Brussels

Boris and Allegra married at St Michael and All Angels, West Felton on 5 September 1987. While she looked stunning, Boris failed to find anything suitable to wear and had to be lent a pair of trousers by Tory MP John Biffen. Unfortunately, his shoes did not fit and Boris had to keep on his own battered footwear.

At the reception at Woodhouse, the composer Hans Werner Henze – a gay German Marxist – gave the world premiere of his piece "Allegra e Boris". His previous compositions had lauded Che Guevara and Ho Chi Minh. Anna Steiger, daughter of Claire Bloom and Rod Steiger, sang an aria from *The Marriage of Figaro*. The confetti were sugared almonds.

Rings were exchanged but, by lunchtime, Boris had mysteriously lost his. He had also lost the wedding certificate which was found, months later, in the pocket of Biffen's trousers. Reflecting on his own youthful marriage, Stanley remarked they were "lambs to the slaughter".

Allegra is thought to have paid for their honeymoon in Egypt. They then bought a flat in a converted Victorian house in Olympia, west London. Boris took a well-paid job with a high-flying management consultancy and bought a pair of red braces, standard kit in the post-Big Bang City of London. He was not well suited to the job.

"Try as I might, I could not look at an overhead projection of a growth profit matrix, and stay conscious," he said.

Boris stayed just long enough to collect his joining fee and, after a week, left. But he was so well connected that, with the highest recommendations, he walked straight into *The Times* as a graduate trainee. They sent him on a three-month secondment to the *Express & Star* in Wolverhampton to learn the business of reporting.

Allegra's own journalistic career, spent largely on the *Evening Standard*'s Londoner's Diary column, was soon to have a setback. She and Boris had written a piece for the *Sunday Telegraph* about Olivia Channon, daughter of Trade and Industry Secretary Paul Channon, who had choked on her own vomit in the Oxford rooms of Gottfried von Bismarck. It included details of a lunch where Tina Brown, who in 1984 had moved from editing the *Tatler* in London to *Vanity Fair* in New York, tried to extract the "tasteless details" of Olivia's death. The piece appeared under Allegra's by-line, but it was Boris who had been at the lunch. That allowed Tina Brown to dismiss the whole article as fiction. Allegra quit journalism.

Boris returned to London without a good report from the West Midlands. *The Times* moved him onto the desk rewriting copy from the news agencies. On his one opportunity to visit the frontline – a National Union of Seamen's strike in Dover – Boris fled back to the newspaper's Wapping headquarters at the first opportunity.

More trouble ensued when an archaeological dig in London unearthed the lost palace of Edward II, where Boris said that the King had cavorted with his catamite Piers Gaveston, quoting, ostensibly, his godfather Dr Colin Lucas of Balliol. However, Gaveston was executed in 1312 and the palace was not built until 1325. Lucas, who was aiming for a professorship in Chicago as a stepping stone to the vice-chancellorship of Oxford, had not been interviewed and protested that he would not have made such an elementary mistake.

Boris wriggled on the hook, but it was plain that he had made up the quote – a sacking offence on *The Times* in the 1980s. Boris still blames "fact-grubbing historians" for his downfall. Nevertheless, through Max Hastings, he walked straight into a job as a leader writer on the *Daily Telegraph*. It was Boris's spiritual home.

He was no newsman though. Boris had attended the wedding of Earl Spencer, along with the Prince and Princess of Wales. The Peterborough column heard that best man Darius Guppy had failed to deliver the traditional speech. When Boris was asked to confirm this, he "blustered [and] did the wobbly blancmange act".

However, when called upon, he would sweep aside the coffee cups, sandwich wrappings and papers that cluttered his desk and, occasionally strutting up and down, produced seamless copy to a deadline, so clear he was in his opinions.

"I've only seen a few people – Max Hastings, A.N. Wilson and Robert Fox – write like that under pressure," said features writer Bernice Davison. "It's an amazing feat of concentration, being able to produce 1,200 or 1,500 flowing words without a trace of the angst it would cause most of us."

Meanwhile junior staff and undergraduates on work experience were dragooned to bring coffee, tea, sandwiches and research material. And Boris spent his time honing his unique style. He does not pepper his column with Woosteresque anachronisms such as "crumbs" and "cripes", though there is that perception of him which he does little to challenge. However, he addresses his readers as "my friends", as if co-opting them. His enemies are also addressed as "my friend", to disparaging effect.

True, he plays the fogey, but his pieces are cleverly crafted. He takes a specific event from his slightly elevated lifestyle, or an object, such as a worn out ski glove, then weaves a story out of it, usually one that charms those of a right wing persuasion. The story is used to illustrate a point that is, for a dyed-in-the-wool Conservative, slightly left-wing in its sentiment. He is marvellously inclusive. Here is the fool making a sensible, well-argued point, and a standard-bearer for the right, making a point that would not sit badly with a bleeding-heart leftie. For example, while the rest of the Conservative Party run scared of Nigel Farage on immigration, Boris shrugs and says that, while some people are naturally afraid of it, we need to get used to it. It is the consequence and wellspring of Britain's success.

However, Boris's pieces were frequently spiked because they were late. He also liked to play the fool around the office. So in 1989, he was sent to the *Telegraph's* bureau in Brussels. He knew the city, having spent some of his childhood there, and could speak good French and Italian, along with some German and Spanish. The salary was good, but Boris insisted on extra money for uprooting his wife. When she had finished her law exams that summer, Allegra followed him to Brussels – after all, he needed someone to do his washing and cleaning. Otherwise, she saw little of him.

To start with, the posting seemed a poisoned chalice. News emanating from the Brussels bureaucracy was by and large dull. But then Mrs Thatcher took up cudgels against the EU and the Berlin Wall fell, along with the Soviet Union. The re-unification of Germany was about to redraw the map of Europe and Boris was the man on the spot.

As a reporter, Boris was hopelessly out of his depth, but other members of the press corps were happy to lend a hand. His father still lived and worked in Brussels and could engineer key introductions. Geoff Meade, from the Press Association wire service, recalled being invited to Sunday lunch by Stanley. During aperitifs, a taxi crunched to a halt in the driveway and out jumped the stunning Allegra and Boris in the world's loudest pair of Bermuda shorts. In a city known for its sober elegance, Boris was known for his eccentric attire.

Seeing him in one particularly shabby suit, one French journalist enquired: "*Qui est ce monstre?*"

When nothing else worked, Boris fell back on clowning. At press conferences, he would ask questions in comically bad French, even though he could speak the language well. He was always on show. Even when he darted around Brussels in his bright red Alfa Romeo with its doors held on with string, he had AC/DC blaring on the stereo. He demanded attention.

Boris soon spotted that the EU press corps was rather too cosy with the bureaucrats they were reporting on and went out of his way to shake things up. He took up the Eurosceptic cause, which had formerly belonged to Tony Benn and those on the left. Boris made Euroscepticism the property of the right, largely by making fun of the EU's decisions and institutions.

"Changes in the rules governing crisps and sausages could so easily symbolize the threat posed by Brussels to the British way of life," he wrote.

"EC cheese row takes the biscuit," ran one headline.

Egged on by Max Hasting, who urged him to "be more pompous", he was the acknowledged master of the "straight banana" school of EU reporting, and his stories became essential reading for Mrs Thatcher as well as other journalists. Other newspapers carried stories about him. He even had influence, though it was acknowledged that his stories were not always accurate.

Well known for not being the most assiduous checker of facts, Boris was fed a wholly untrue rumour to see if it surfaced in a Johnson story. It did.

He even announced that the commission headquarters in Brussels was to be blown up after asbestos had been found. Blowing it up would only have spread the danger. Instead, the building was extensively refitted and still stands.

His favourite target was Jacques Delors, president of the European Commission from 1985 to 1995. After the signing of the Maastricht treaty, but before it was ratified by the member states, the *Sunday Telegraph* ran a speculative piece by Boris on the front page under the headline "Delors Plan to Rule Europe".

"Cor, I thought," Boris wrote later. "That was a bold way of expressing it, and I wasn't sure that my chums in the EC commission would be thrilled. But the splash was the splash – the main article on the front page – and I happily consented. That story went down big. It may not have caused the dropping of marmalade over the breakfast tables of England, but it was huge in Denmark. With less than a month until their referendum, and with mounting paranoia about the erosion of Danish independence, the story was seized on by the 'No' campaign. They photocopied it a thousandfold. They marched the streets of Copenhagen with my story fixed to their banners. And on June 2, a spectacularly sunny day, they joyously rejected the treaty and derailed the project. Jacques Delors was not the only victim of the disaster; the aftershocks were felt across Europe, and above all in Britain."

The no vote was a body-blow to Delors. At a press conference afterwards, it was said "the pallor of his skin suggested he had received an electric shock".

Delors tried to fight back, but Boris's wit gave him the upper hand.

"We answer his attacks," said one frustrated EU official, "but the problem is that our answers are not funny."

Politicians feared the press conferences he attended and tried to "Boris-proof" their policies. It is even thought that Foreign Secretary Douglas Hurd put pressure on Max Hastings to have him sacked. Hurd has denied this, but claimed to have chummed up with fellow Eton King's Scholar "to keep him off my back". Boris reciprocated with vitriolic attacks. The Foreign Office was said to have dedicated a team to rebutting his stories, or having them spiked in the first place.

While the government struggled to maintain its position in Europe, Boris always managed to put it on the back foot. After a long day's negotiation, Hurd always dreaded the press conference afterwards with Boris there in the front row, preparing to throw a grenade.

Then came the most seismic political event in Boris's world – the ignominious ousting of Margaret Thatcher.

"After it was all over, my wife Marina, claimed she came upon me stumbling down a street in Brussels, tears in my eyes, and claiming that it was as if someone had shot Nanny," he wrote later. "I dispute this…"

As well he might, as he never had a nanny and he was still married to Allegra at the time. But people who knew him always took his stories with a pinch of salt. He was not a person of conviction like Thatcher, nor was he nearly as Eurosceptic as he made himself out to be – particularly because his father worked for the Commission. Far from being anti-European, Boris was suspected of being a closet federalist.

It was an act. He would work himself up for bilious rants by locking himself in his office and hurling a torrent of abuse at his yucca plant. Once he had achieved peak frenzy, he would rattle out his piece at machine-gun speed, beating the keys with his fist. If anyone interrupted, he would yell furious expletives at them.

Back in Britain, these rants were stoking the Euro debate that was tearing the Conservative Party under John Major apart. Boris later explained on *Desert Island Discs*: "I was sort of chucking these rocks over the garden wall and I listened to this amazing crash from the greenhouse next over in England as everything I wrote from Brussels was having this amazing, explosive effect on the Tory Party. And it really gave me this, I suppose, rather weird sense of power."

This would eventually make the party that he supported unelectable for over a decade.

John Major accused Boris of being obsessed with Europe. It was true. His war with Delors consumed him, leaving little time for a home life. Often he would jump on a plane in pursuit of a story. Allegra would have to phone the foreign desk of the *Telegraph* to find out where he was.

"You get past caring and you start drinking malt whisky," she said. And she feared she was going to have a nervous breakdown.

The straw that broke the camel's back was when Boris came home one night and asked her what she thought about "subsidiarity" – the latest entry to Euro-lexicon. She packed her bags and flew back to London.

Boris was distraught. In the aftermath, he was seen drunk. It was very rare for him to even have more than a few glasses of wine, though often he would use a mythical "hangover" as an excuse for lateness or ill-preparedness – then he could fire off with his mind as sharp as ever.

Normally not a clubbable person, Boris turned to his colleagues for support. This was a surprise for them. He was usually very secretive, never known to open up. While other journalists hunted in packs, Boris was a lone wolf and his aloofness was often taken for arrogance.

Chapter Six – Boris Unbound

While the divorce was in progress, there was a reconciliation. Allegra had begun studying for her Law Society finals, but flew over to Brussels at the weekends. Then she enrolled at the Université Libra de Bruxelles for a Masters in EU law. This had been recommended to her by Boris's old school-chum Marina Wheeler, who had taken the course the previous year.

Not only had he been enamoured of her when they were at the European School together, they had dated briefly when they were sixteen. He had discovered that you could get a free lunch at the Hare Krishna centre in Soho.

"I thought the food was delicious, but she didn't think much of it and has never forgiven me," said Boris.

She was a public school girl too, but had gone to the laid-back co-educational Bedales whose alumni included Sophie Dahl, Gyles Brandreth and Daniel Day-Lewis. Then she studied Law at Fitzwilliam College, Cambridge

Marina was living nearby in Brussels and Allegra would invite her around for dinner. But when Allegra was away, Boris began pursuing her. He was not a man who could manage on his own and he always craved female company. Though Marina was a left-winger and Boris's high Tory views were an anathema to her, she found herself falling in love with him.

Soon after Allegra left for good, Marina fell pregnant. By then she and Boris were engaged. They seemed a better match. While Allegra had sought to change Boris, Marina accepted him the way he was.

Despite Boris's general ineptitude with paperwork, the divorce was rushed through. Marina and Boris married in Horsham town hall and had a low-key reception in the garden of the Wheelers' house nearby. It could hardly have been more different from his first wedding. Marina kept her maiden name and the honeymoon was one night in a hotel in East Grinstead. He had been a bachelor for just twelve days.

Back in Brussels, they moved into a house. But otherwise things had not changed. When Marina went into labour she had to call the *Telegraph*'s foreign desk in London to track him down. Boris was at the coast, covering the story of a ship that looked like it might sink and he insisted on filing it before flying to the side of his wife. He celebrated the birth with a piece headed "Congratulations! It's a Belgian."

As both Boris and Marina had been born abroad, their daughter did not automatically inherit their nationality. In the article he begged the Home Secretary Michael Howard not to let her become a Belgian by default, saying: "Do you wish to see her claimed by a nation which refused to sell us ammunition in the Gulf war? Shall she scamper, her face gleaming with chips and mayonnaise, as thousands of Bruxellois did the other day, to watch the National Day firework display, her heart beating at the sight of the black-red-yellow flags?" She was registered as a British subject five years later.

Marina wanted to call their daughter Lara; Boris preferred Lettice. As a result, she was christened Lara Lettice, but is known as Lara. Fatherhood did not dent Boris's 24/7 work schedule and he was as driven as ever, writing for the *Telegraph*, the *Sunday Telegraph* and their sister publication, the *Spectator*.

In one piece, he rued the state of the modern British male – "his reluctance or inability to take control of his woman and be head of a household". *Private Eye* carried a repost, saying: "These moral lectures sound a little odd when one learns that Johnson had to arrange a quickie divorce from his first wife, Allegra Mostyn-Owen, after discovering that he had impregnated his lover, Marina Wheeler. Johnson's belief that a man should take charge in the household scarcely tallies which his own domestic habits. He is notoriously reluctant to pay for anything (he wasn't even prepared to foot the bill for his first honeymoon) and is almost incapable of dealing with income tax, insurance policies and other such duties that often fall to the head of the household. 'The modern British male,' Johnson concluded in the *Spectator* last week, 'is useless.' Speak for yourself, matey."

The source for this story was, allegedly, Allegra herself.

Others confirmed his meanness. He did not buy drinks or take people to lunch, and acquaintances were warned never to lend him money as he did not pay it back. He was also eager to borrow – or lift – other people's stories, give them his own spin and outshine the original with his splash, but got away with it with flattery and charm.

After four years in Brussels, Boris's charm was wearing a little thin on both EU officials and other journalists. As he packed his bags, James Landale of *The Times* wrote a valedictory modelled on Hilaire Belloc's "Matilda", about a girl who tells lies:

Boris told such dreadful lies

It made one gasp and stretch one's eyes.

His desk, which from its earliest youth

Had kept a strict regard for truth,

Attempted to believe each scoop

Until the landed in the soup.

In the parody, Boris says that Britain is going to pull out of the EU, and the other correspondents have to follow his lead as there is no time to check the facts, then are forced to retract when Douglas Hurd and John Major deny it. Then the other journalists become sceptical.

For every time he said "Delors' the Messiah",

We only answered: "Nah, it's a flyer."

In journalist speak, a flyer is a speculative piece based on guesswork rather than facts. The lampoon concludes:

The moral is, it is indeed.

It might be wrong but it's a damn fine read.

Boris sent a note, thanking Landale for the poem.

Back in London, Boris began looking for a new stage on which to parade his talents. He fancied becoming a war correspondent, but the *Telegraph* decided that his habit of being economical with the truth might prove dangerous in a combat zone. Besides, Boris was a notoriously big spender on his expense account and sending him somewhere where he could not be reined in might bankrupt the paper.

Even the column he got reviewing cars on *GQ* was said to be the most expensive in magazine history. He would casually double-park the latest high-powered "babe magnet" outside the Royal Festival Hall or New Scotland Yard. As a result, parking fines would build up "like drifting snow on the windshield". More than once, a junior had to be sent around to fetch it back from the car pound.

Back in London, Boris wanted to live in Notting Hill where Rachel lived. It was soon to be home to David Cameron and other up-and-coming Tories. But, at Marina's insistence, they bought a house in Islington, home to Tony Blair and New Labour.

Illustrating the political gulf between them, when asked how he formulated his right-wing ideas, Boris said he asked what Marina and her family thought on any subject then turned 180 degrees – "I can't go wrong."

Although they were living in what Boris would consider enemy territory, that area of Islington was a "media gulch", full of TV producers and journalists, though usually of a liberal bent. And while the area is affluent and gentrified, it was close to the bad lands of Holloway, so crime was an ever-present worry.

Marina had given their new house a contemporary look with stripped-pine floors, while Boris contributed the old-fashioned mess. When an American journalist came to do an interview for *Vanity Fair*, he found Boris in his underwear, bumbling around looking for his trousers. Suspecting that the scene may have been contrived, Boris, he wrote, "quite clearly invites underestimation".

The Johnsons needed a large house. Their first son, Milo Arthur, was born in 1995, Cassia Peaches in 1997 and Theodore Apollo in 1999 – these last two had their father's colouring, while Milo and Lara were honey blondes. None of them inherited any of their mother's dark, half-Indian looks.

The children went to Canonbury Primary. When Boris played celebrity auctioneer at the school fundraiser, other local celebs contributed lots that included Chris Martin of Coldplay playing in your living room and a guided tour of the House of Lords by Lord Adonis. The event raised tens of thousands.

Not that Boris was uncritical.

"I have children in state primary education, and I have to tell you that times have changed," he wrote. "They call the teachers by their first names, which was not the case when I was in state primary education. The teachers have no power whatsoever to discipline them, terrified as they are of the great engine of state retribution if they are felt in any way to have infringed the rights of the child."

When it came to secondary schooling, Boris was not embarrassed to go private, though he admitted that the middle-class flight from state education compounded the problems of the schools they left behind.

Naturally, Boris wanted to send his sons to Eton. But Marina put her foot down. She did not want another Old Etonian in the house and her doggedness had a profound influence on his thinking. For example, when Lord Macpherson of Cluny's report into the death of Stephen Lawrence found "institutional racism" in the Metropolitan Police, Boris dismissed this, at first, as "Orwellian" – in, of all places, the *Guardian*.

A year later, he wrote in the *Spectator*: "I have had savage arguments with my nearest and dearest, and, slowly, I have begun to see things his way … The Laird of Cluny is no loony."

Boris so frequently lost to the liberal-left arguments of Marina in the domestic debating chamber that he began calling her "M'learned wife", while she called him her "fifth child".

In the *Evening Standard*, Boris claimed to be a "careerist nappy-changing MP-cum-journalist-cum-househusband", but it is clear that most domestic chores are left up to Marina, who also has a high-powered career as a lawyer to maintain. Not for him "ridiculous compulsorily paid paternity leave".

Admittedly, with their joint salaries, the Johnson's could afford to hire a house keeper, cleaner, a nanny and a couple of au pairs.

Boris's musings on whether women really want to work so hard, and blaming women graduates for everything from the rise in house prices to mugging, drew the charge of sexism.

"Obviously a Neanderthal corner of my heart worries about some aspects of the coming feminization," he admitted. "Will we all become even more namby-pamby, elf-n-safety-conscious, regulation-prone and generally incapable of beating the Australians at anything than we already are?"

The children did not see much of their workaholic father, but when they did it was fun. A *Sun* reader snapped him test driving a 195mph Lamborghini Gallardo Spyder for *GQ* magazine with his two sons in the front seat of the sports car. He took his rugby-mad son Milo to Twickenham, played tennis with the boys on a Sunday morning and, when a family holiday to Greece was nearly scuppered when they turned up late at Luton airport, Boris jumped on a windowsill in the departure lounge and made a cash offer for tickets, eventually parting with £2,000 for two extra seats they needed on the EasyJet to Athens.

Boris was criticized by fellow parents for being "eccentrically liberal" by letting his children watch the James Bond movie *For Your Eyes Only*. He compounded the charge by admitting that they also watched *Hot Fuzz* and *Shaun of the Dead*. But then one of Boris's frequent targets are Puritans.

The Johnsons' attitude to parenting was outlined in a book of verse called *Perils of the Pushy Parent – A Cautionary Tale*, written and illustrated by Boris. It continues such gems as:

Loving parents, learn from me.

If your children crave TV

Tell them, OK, what the hell

You can watch it for a spell…

IF YOU READ A BOOK AS WELL.

The *Guardian* called it "the most cringe-making book every published". Boris's next-door neighbour in Islington was Ian Katz, then a senior editor at the *Guardian*. Boris would make regular protests about his treatment by that left-leaning newspaper by leaving his copy on Katz's doorstep.

But Boris was not that liberal a parent. He came out against Nintendo, Game Boy and PlayStation, citing "the catastrophic effect these blasted gizmos are having on the literacy and the prospects of young males".

"They sit for so long that their souls seem to have been sucked down the cathode ray tube," he said. "Steel yourself for the screams and yank out that plug," he urged. "And if they still kick up a fuss, then get out the sledgehammer and strike a blow for literacy."

Chapter Seven – Blond Ambition

Boris's despatches from Brussels had damaged the Conservative government. He enjoyed all the attention this brought him in what he admitted was a "babyish way". There was factional fighting between the pro- and anti-Europe wings of the Conservatives and the whole party was mired in "Tory sleaze".

Boris had had his own brush with scandal. Darius Guppy and a business partner had themselves tied up in a New York hotel room, making it look like they had been robbed of £1.8-million jewels in an insurance fraud. When Stuart Collier from the *News of the World* looked into the case, Guppy called Boris asking for Collier's address so he could have him beaten up. Boris did not give him the address, but the call was on tape and he seemed sympathetic to his friend's plan. When Guppy was jailed for the insurance scam, Boris still praised him in the *Telegraph* for living "by his own Homeric code of honour, loyalty and revenge". Soon after a tape of the telephone conversation was sent to Max Hastings, Boris was summoned and chastised. Only later did a transcript appear in the *Mail on Sunday*. By this time, Boris was a forthright champion of law and order. He told the *Mail* that it was "all a bit of a joke".

At the age of just thirty, Boris was made an assistant editor on the *Telegraph* and chief political columnist.

"I'm a bit worried," said Boris about the appointment. "I don't have any political opinions."

When pushed, all he could come up with was: "Well, I'm against Europe and against capital punishment."

The new editor, Charles Moore, said that Boris performed the task with "maximum idleness". Paul Goodman, former *Telegraph* comment editor, recalled an editorial meeting where Boris was asked what he was going to write that day.

"Aaaarrrrgggghhh! Cripes! Erm …" said Boris.

"Well?"

"I thought … sort of … eeerrrhhhmmm."

"Sorry?"

"I mean … um … Blair."

"What about him?"

"Sort of … gosh! … Europe … and …"

"And?"

"Hague … I mean, Hague! … er … sort of …"

"So, I'm to tell the editor that you're writing about sort of Blair, Europe and Hague, sort of?"

"No … well … un … Yah! … er … That's it!"

Nevertheless, a few hours later, an "immaculately composed and piratically arresting essay would appear".

On another occasion, he asked Northern Ireland Unionist leader David Trimble a typically waffling question at a crucial Belfast peace conference and Trimble replied: "Fuck off Boris."

But he found always found something both amusing and trenchant to fill his column. Now up to speed on everything European, he found a worthy adversary in Tony Blair's spin doctor Alastair Campbell and, in 1997, won "Commentator of the Year" at the "What the Papers Say" awards.

However, having Boris annoying people out in Brussels was one thing, having him bumbling around the *Telegraph*'s building in London was quite another. He began to get on people's nerves. Even his use of language was guaranteed to grate. He talked of "coolies" and "piccaninnies". The problem with Africa was "not that we were once in charge, but that we are not in charge anymore," he said. Even in the face of the credit crunch, he defended the rich.

"We seem to have forgotten that societies need rich people, even sickeningly rich people, and not just to provide jobs for those who clean swimming pools and resurface tennis courts," he wrote. "Without them there would be no Chatsworth or Longleat."

Like a posh version of Jeremy Clarkson, he set out to offend virtually everyone, but got away with it through wit and charm.

"Islam will only be truly acculturated to our way of life when you could expect a Bradford audience to roll in the aisles at *Monty Python's Life of Mohammed*," he said.

"They say [Tony Blair] is shortly off to the Congo. No doubt the AK47s will fall silent, and the pangas will stop their hacking of human flesh, and the tribal warriors will all break out in watermelon smiles to see the big white chief touch down in his big white British taxpayer-funded bird."

"Do you really mean to say the [British] empire wasn't a good thing? … The best fate for Africa would be if the old colonial powers, or their citizens, scrambled once again in her direction; on the understanding that this time they will not be asked to feel guilty."

Palestine? "If we were Israelis … we would dispatch an American-built ground-assault helicopter and blow the place to bits. Then we would send in bulldozers to scrape over the remains, and we would do the same to all the other houses in the area … this is the best way to deter Palestinian families from nurturing these vipers in their bosoms, and also the best way of explaining to the death-hungry narcissists that they may get the 72 black-eyed virgins of scripture, but their family gets the bulldozer."

Then there was: "Whenever George Dubya Bush appears on television, with his buzzard squint and his Ronald Reagan side-nod, I find a cheer rising irresistibly in my throat." However, he later reined back, saying: "It's just maddening that when asked to form a simple declarative sentence on child literacy the leader of the free world is less articulate than my seven-year-old."

And at a Gay Pride dinner, he said: "I'm delighted that as of this autumn any young man will be able to take his chum up the Arcelor Orbit and marry him." Elsewhere, for football fans, it was "up the Arsenal".

"The chicks in the GQ expenses department – and if you can't call them chicks, then what the hell, I ask you, is the point of writing for GQ." In the *Spectator*, he claimed to have invented the Tottometer – "the Geiger-counter that detects good-looking women".

Like Clarkson, Boris built a constituency on television. Both have appeared on *Have I Got News For You?* On his first appearance as a panellist in 1998 the Darius Guppy tape was sprung on him. In the *Spectator*, he complained of being "stitched up" and called the show a fraud, claiming that, while appearing to be ad-lib, the lines were meticulously prepared.

Nevertheless, he quickly made up with fellow panellist Ian Hislop, editor of *Private Eye*, who said of his complaining column: "What a load of bollocks, Boris – you must have knocked that out in twenty minutes."

"No, it was shorter than that," Boris replied.

"I expect you were pissed as well," said Hislop.

"I might have been," said Boris. One of his familiar tactics was to disarm the critic by admitting the charge, even when he was not guilty.

The next time he appeared on the show he made an endearing apology. Then he faced a barrage of questions about Iain Duncan Smith, then Conservative Party leader. Boris could not answer a single one of them, which made him all the more endearing.

In the wings, he once asked Hislop: "Do you know what the Tory policy is on immigration?"

Hislop said he didn't.

"Neither do I," said Boris.

When he was asked to be a guest presenter, he pulled it off in typical bumbling fashion. According to Hislop, most presenters spent two days rehearsing. Boris "turned up at six p.m. on the day and had never read the script, which he proceeded to read in that dazed way of his. His insouciance was extremely funny."

Again he used self-deprecation to win the audience over.

"My speaking style was criticized by no less an authority than Arnold Schwarzenegger. It was a low moment, my friends, to have my rhetorical skills denounced by a monosyllabic Austrian cyborg."

On one occasion, his mobile phone rang. He answered it, saying: "I can't talk now, I'm on the television."

Some suspect that this, too, was contrived. Making no apology for his seeming incompetence, Boris said that the real shocker was "not that people are so foolish as to appear on TV, but that people are so idle as to watch it."

Besides, he got £1,000 a time, which was enough to take his kids skiing. And he realized that to succeed he had to appear on shows that people actually wanted to watch; otherwise, "you just stick on Andrew Neil's late-night yawn-a-thon, then you're never going to get anywhere".

His other credits include *Parkinson*, *Question Time*, *Breakfast with Frost* and *Top Gear*. He even had his own two-part TV series, *Boris Johnson and the Dream of Rome*, where he tried to discover how the ancient Romans managed to run a united empire and why the European Union has failed to pull off the same feat. Even when he was being erudite about ancient history – could any other politician do that? – Boris kept the trademark haystack hair which is deliberately messed up immediately before the cameras roll.

The television brought him to a wider audience. He also got star treatment at the paper. Charles Moore would ring him half-an-hour before deadline to find he had not even started his column – or even decided what it was going to be about. He often delivered late, but somehow persuaded the editor to put it in. It was, perhaps, lucky Boris wrote so seamlessly that his copy needed little editing. Nor did he like his prose being tampered with. He typically delivered fifty words short of the required length, so that no one could take a word out.

Boris, of course, made light of his tardiness.

"Dark Forces dragged me away from the keyboard, swirling forces of irresistible force and power," he quipped.

Boris was also inept at his other duty, commissioning comment pieces when Simon Heffer was away. To complete his own column, other journalists found their brains comprehensively picked.

On the few occasions he was put in charge of the paper when Charles Moore was not there, Boris wandered around looking completely baffled. He had not bothered to find out what the job entailed and assumed that, like a well-oiled machine, the paper would run itself. Essentially, he depended on others to do the job for him. Once he even gave a memory stick along with an email address to a complete stranger at an airport and got him to file his copy for him.

There is one thing you can depend on Boris for, Charles Moore once said, and that is to let you down. That was partly because the affable Boris will always say yes to things he had no intention of doing. And he always got away with it with a handful of jokes and ladles full of charm.

Despite his joking around, Boris longed to be taken seriously and had long harboured political ambitions. Since 1993, he had been looking for a seat, initially in the European Parliament, but John Major threatened to veto his candidacy. Then in 1997 he stood as Tory candidate in the unwinnable seat of Clwyd South, dutifully learning the Welsh national anthem and how to order fish and chips in Welsh. He read up on farming and the Common Agricultural Policy, and even won some admirers in the local constituency. Nevertheless, his efforts were doomed.

"I fought Clwyd South, as we candidates put it – and Clwyd South fought back," he said later.

That was the year the Conservative Party suffered its worst defeat since 1906. However, the big beasts of the Tory party who had been rattled by Boris's Eurosceptic attacks from Brussels began to leave the stage, and in 2000 he was selected for Michael Heseltine's rock solid Conservative seat of Henley. For this he had to thank Andrew Mitchell, who eventually fell from power in "Plebgate".

There was one slight problem with his selection. In 1999, Boris had been appointed editor of the *Spectator* on the condition that he would give up looking for a seat in parliament. When proprietor Conrad Black discovered a couple of months later that Boris had sought selection in two different constituencies, he hauled him in and asked him to explain himself.

Boris resorted to his old tactic of simply coming out with his hands up. He admitted that his conduct was outrageous and that Black was within his rights to sack him. He went on to convince Black that he could edit the magazine and be an MP at the same time. Black succumbed to his charm.

As Boris himself said: "My policy on cake is pro having it and pro eating it."

Others were worried that Boris was up to the job of being editor in the first place – even without the added responsibility of representing a constituency. Journalist Andrew Grimson said making Boris editor of the *Spectator* was like "entrusting a Ming vase to an ape". Boris made him the magazine's foreign editor, an unpaid position that allowed him to file copy from as far away as Hackney and Surbiton – and, on one occasion, Burnley.

Prime Minister Tony Blair had called Boris to Number Ten to congratulate him personally on this appointment. Perhaps he thought Boris would continue the demolition job on the Conservative Party he had begun in Brussels.

BBC Radio Four's *The Week in Westminster* almost immediately dropped him as a presenter. Boris claimed that it was because he had a posh voice and "lacked the chameleon skills of Tony Blair who knows how to perform the perfect glottal stop and drop an aitch on *Richard and Judy*."

Black's chief executive Dan Colson was also angry that Boris had persistently lied to him, saying that he was not seeking a parliamentary seat. After Colson had vented his spleen, Boris convinced him that he could edit the magazine part-time. After all, with all his other media commitments, that was what he was doing anyway. Indeed, one of his first acts as editor had been to take two weeks paternity leave. He continued writing columns for the *Telegraph*, *GQ*, appearing on radio and TV, and writing the novel *Seventy Two Virgins*, which was published in 2005.

However, with Boris's hand on the tiller, sales of the *Spectator* were already climbing and it was making money. So Colson sent in minders, including old Fleet Street hand Stuart Reid who made sure the magazine came out on time. And when things went wrong, Boris was not around to shoulder the blame.

"Quite easy, this magazine editing lark," Boris was overheard saying.

Life at the *Spectator*'s Doughty Street offices was like a war room during a major crisis, with Boris missing interviews, speeches and deadlines and often with people dragooning to cover for him at the last moment. Sometimes, at the eleventh hour, when there was no alternative, he would dash off a piece himself.

"Because I have no time to do it, I do it in no time – you just whack it out," he told the *New York Times*.

The show was kept on the road by Boris's Yorkshire-born secretary Ann Sindall, who played "pantomime Northerner" to his "pantomime toff". She dealt with unpaid bills, parking tickets, complaints, tax demands, members of the Johnson household and fended off people trying to find out where he was – even sewing up a rip in his trousers on one occasion. She did all this, it was said, "with the implacable demeanour of a headmistress trained by the SAS".

Amidst this chaos, Boris said he had "more fun than is strictly proper". He rarely came in before lunchtime. There were long, liquid lunches, pretty young women and ping pong in the garden. Editorial meetings were largely an opportunity to swap jokes. The door to the editor's office was always open for anyone who wanted to read the paper or just have a lie down. Above it all was a bust of the Athenian statesman Pericles.

Although the *Spectator* is the voice of Conservatism, Boris allowed all shades of opinion to flourish, even employing the left-wing cartoonist Steve Bell from the *Guardian* whose work he much admired. Irate leftie Rod Liddle also had his say. Against this, Boris kept on Greek-born journalist Taki Theodoracopulos, whose casual racism in his "High Life" column even drew complaints from Conrad Black.

Boris himself ran a leader under the headline "Long Live Elitism", saying: "Without elites and elitism, man would still be in the caves." But in turn he stuck up for asylum seekers and economic migrants. He also hired Andrew Gilligan, who left the BBC after he had claimed that the British Government had "sexed up" a report on weapons of mass destruction to exaggerate the capabilities of Saddam Hussein in the run-up to the Iraq war.

Veteran theatre critic Sheridan Morley was fired in favour of Oxford chum Toby Young who said he knew nothing about the theatre. Earl Spencer penned a diary. Nicky Haslam, Anna Ford and

Joan Collins all contributed, along with numerous members of the Johnson clan, including sister Rachel, brothers Leo and Jo, father Stanley, father-in-law Charles Wheeler and brother-in-law Ivo Dawnay, along with Paul Johnson and Frank Johnson who are not related.

Though getting a good salary himself, Boris was notoriously parsimonious when it came to paying his contributors. Five hundred pounds was top whack, but pieces were to be short. They were to take no more than forty-five minutes and three calls.

When an undercover reporter from the *News of the World* ensnared the Earl of Hardwicke into supplying cocaine, which got him suspended from the Conservative Party, Boris struck back by getting his chum Lloyd Evans to sell the tabloid the inside story of the drug den at the *Spectator*, with Boris himself as both a dealer and a heavy user. The *NoW* smelt a rat.

Evans was then taken on as poetry editor with a salary of one case of cheap plonk every six months. To make ends meet, Evans sold a story to the *Mail on Sunday* about a group of greens having lunch at the *Spectator*. House rules were that the guest list was secret, encouraging diners to speak freely. One of the guests, Zac Goldsmith, complained. Boris phoned Evans to upbraid him.

"Here's the bad news," he said. "You're fired as poetry editor."

There was a pause.

"Now the good news – you're reinstated."

Evans was even promoted.

Boris, the arch rule-breaker, liked journalism to incite. When David Gardner of the *Financial Times* filed a piece on Hindu fundamentalism, Boris told him to "give it more oomph".

"I want to see newsagents go up in flames," he said.

Boris himself outed Dominic Lawson, previous editor of the *Spectator*, as an agent of SIS. When he phoned to complain, Boris said: "I just did it for a laugh."

There were other problems with the sister publication, the *Telegraph*, who were supposed to have the first option on any *Spectator* article. Instead, Boris would sell any likely piece to the *Daily Mail*. When Colson called Boris to complain, Boris eventually phoned back to say: "I cannot believe I've been so monumentally stupid. I should be immediately sacked, my pay confiscated retrospectively, marched out to the square outside Canary Wharf, hung, draw and quartered on the flagstaff." Colson could not get a word in.

Conrad Black got the same treatment. When he called to complain about an article, Boris said: "I am on the top of the most dangerous piste in Gstaad, staring into the face of death, about to decide, depending on why you are calling me, if my intention is to survive my next run or not."

Sometimes things got out of hand. When Petronella Wyatt launched an attack on the Marian Fathers' Polish boarding school at Fawley Court, it drew protests from the Polish ambassador, Catholics and local bigwigs. But Fawley Court was on the borders of his Henley constituency and the election was just nine months away, so he sent out scores of grovelling letters and went to apologize in person.

With the election less than a month away, Boris set his sights on a larger target – Edward Heath, the Tory Prime Minister that had taken Britain into the EEC before getting bumped by Margaret Thatcher.

"It would be utterly magnificent if I could tell you, my friends, that Sir Edward, at 84, has got over his Incredible Sulk and become a piping geyser of optimism about the party under whose banner I am about to fight. Alas, amigos, it is not to be," wrote Boris. "From the moment we sit down at the table, with his belly cantilevered between us like some decked whale, it is clear that he is in no mood to boost my morale … Here we are, two fat Balliol blonds, and the older one wants to rock the confidence of the younger. Well, I won't let him."

Chapter Eight – Bo Selecta

Boris was not a shoo-in at Henley. The Europhile Heseltine certainly did not want to give up his seat to the standard-bearer of Euroscepticism. However, because of his notoriety on *Have I Got News For You?*, the president of the local branch of the Conservative Party invited him to stand. Boris's application came in a week late. Nevertheless, it was accepted.

The front-runner was lawyer David Platt, who was considered to be on the Conservative Party fast-track. Then there was leading woman lawyer Jill Andrew. Both were word perfect in party policies and had been tramping the constituency. On the night of the final selection, Boris was nowhere to be found. However, the car park of the hall where the vote was being held was packed with the upmarket cars of those who had come to see him because he was a celebrity. The vote was a forgone conclusion.

Boris was his usual shambling figure but, because he had been to Eton and Oxford, that was all right. When asked a question about the NHS, Boris said that when Marina had been sleeping after giving birth he had eaten his wife's toast. He was disgusted that the nurses were unable to bring her more toast when she woke up. That's why the NHS needed reforming.

And that was it, his only thoughts on a serious issue. But he had delivered the knock-out punch. He had mentioned that he had a wife and children. Rumours were circulating that David Platt, who later married, was gay and that, at university, Jill Andrew had drunk too much and had been a little promiscuous – cardinal sins in the eyes of the members of the Henley Conservative Association. She was even accused of being a friend of Cherie Blair.

After claiming he had no skeletons in the cupboard, Boris was asked about Guppygate.

"This chap felt he had me skewered, and for one terrible millisecond it seemed he might be right," Boris said. "What he forgot was the volatility of the audience and their sense of fair play. His question was so long, and so venomous, and so full of recondite detail about a decade-old non-scandal, that by the end of it I guess some people were rather hoping I'd be able to bat the ball back."

Which he did.

He had been accused of keeping the Guppy business a secret. But he had been questioned about it on a TV show with an audience of millions – "I don't think you could get much more public than that."

The questioner was booed. Later he received abusive letters and was hounded out of the association.

Even so, the selection went to a second vote. But, as the evening dragged on, the ladies of Henley who turned out for Boris stayed on until, finally, the blond bombshell was selected.

Now editing the London *Evening Standard*, Max Hastings changed his Wodehousian analogy, writing a leader warning Boris that: "To maintain his funny man reputation, he will no doubt find himself refining his Bertie Wooster interpretation to the point where the impersonation becomes the man."

But first he would impersonate Heseltine, who had famously brandished the parliamentary mace at left-wingers singing the *Red Flag* in the House of Commons in 1976. Boris did it rather more modestly with Henley Town Council's version at the Mayor's Annual Dinner, guaranteeing him front-page coverage in the *Henley Standard*.

When the election was called in mid–May, Boris ducked out of all his journalistic commitments and went on the stump. His campaign was criticized for being chaotic. But thanks to *Have I Got News For You?*, he was recognized on the doorsteps.

The *Sunday Times'* A.A. Gill, who accompanied him on the campaign trail, said that he eyed a baby as if it were "Sunday lunch". Over sausage and mash, he has a choice of mustard, "English or French – sound or soft on Europe. The knife hovers. Oh dear, he's gone for the French. 'You must come and write for *The Spectator*.' And then he thinks. 'Oh crikey, that's your story, isn't it? How I tried to bribe you with a column on *The Specci*. Damn, damn.'"

Gill concludes: "Boris Johnson is without doubt the very worst putative politician I've ever seen in action. He is utterly, chronically useless – and I can't think of a higher compliment."

Nationwide, the Conservatives did nothing to dent the Labour majority, but Boris won in Henley, albeit with a reduced majority.

"Go back home and prepare for breakfast," he told his supporters.

Covering the count, Anna Ford asked: "How can you expect to look after this constituency when you can't even look after yourself?"

However, the bookies were already giving odds on Boris becoming the next leader of the Conservative Party.

Conrad Black and his wife Barbara Amiel hosted a victory party for him in their Kensington mansion, replete with cardboard cut-outs of Boris. The French ambassador, another guest, compared the event to the cult of Pol Pot.

Boris went on to sell the serialization rights of his book on the campaign, *Friends, Voters, Countrymen: Jottings from the Stump*, to *The Times* – the newspaper that had once sacked him – before offering it to the *Telegraph* that had come to his rescue. Charles Moore was put out as he paid his wages. It was also noted that, when Conrad Black turned up at *Spectator* parties, he passed unnoticed. Boris was the star of the show.

In parliament, things were different though. Another of the new intake was David Cameron, who immediately went onto the prestigious Home Affairs committee, a showcase for new talent. Boris was relegated to the standing committee on Proceeds of Crime Bill, which had 462 clauses to grind through. He was often late – hearings started at nine sharp – or did not turn up at all.

With the Conservative defeat in the election, leader William Hague stepped down. Boris was expected to back Michael Portillo, though Mrs Thatcher had gone cold on him. Boris had once lauded Iain Duncan Smith as the "future of Conservatism". Instead, inexplicably, he backed Europhile Ken Clarke, even throwing the weight of the *Spectator* behind him.

Clarke's opinion was so diametrically opposed to Boris's that this caused some to enquire whether Boris believed in anything. He answered his critics in his 2003 book *Lend Me Your Ears*, saying: "Here, in these articles, is how I think we should be: free-market, tolerant, broadly liberal (though not, perhaps, ultra-libertarian), inclined to see the merit of traditions, anti-regulation, pro-immigrant, pro-standing on your own two feet, pro-alcohol, pro-hunting, pro-motorist and ready to defend to the death the right of Glenn Hoddle to believe in reincarnation."

Although in the House of Commons Boris was now a little fish in a big pond, he was still the editor of the *Spectator*, had his column in the *Telegraph* and appeared regularly on TV – and his motoring column in *GQ* meant that he regularly turned up in the members' car park in a Ferrari or a Bentley. While other members might be jealous, some of his constituents in Henley considered him, because of his other commitments, a part-time MP. Before the election, after all, he had said he would step down from the editorship of the *Spectator* and quit the *Telegraph*. Now he told the *Henley Standard* that he had taken a pay-cut at the *Spectator* because of his reduced role there – though he was still on full salary. His promise to Conrad Black to quit the *Spectator* if he got elected was also broken.

He defended his position by pointing out that both Winston Churchill and Benjamin Disraeli had supported themselves through writing. Like them, he said, he felt destined to lead his country.

Just when the strain was proving too much for him, he discovered the joys of jogging, taking a half-hour run each morning – making a delightful picture for any photo-journalist who might be door-stepping him. He also began to cycle, again showing his genius at re-branding his image. Despite all this exercise, at 5 feet 10, Boris can still swell to 17 stone – not a healthy BMI.

Jogging and cycling further strained his already creaking agenda, but as Boris explained: "The fatal thing is boredom, so I try to have as much on my plate as possible."

This meant he did not have the time, like other new members, to seek advancement working the tearooms and bars of the Palace of Westminster. But he was not very good at schmoozing. That was David Cameron's forte.

What Boris did manage to pull off was to get a large office to himself, rather than share like other members. His staff were housed on the floor below. They were overworked. His secretary Melissa Crawshay-Williams had to cope with a mailbag twice as big as that of other MPs.

In his maiden speech, Boris followed in the parliamentary tradition of praising his predecessor.

"As many in south Oxfordshire and elsewhere have not hesitated to point out, Michael Heseltine is a hard act to follow," he said, "so I approach this moment with much the same sense of self-doubt as Simba in *The Lion King*. For the benefit of those who have not seen Walt Disney's film, there is a poignant moment when Simba, following his father Mufasa across the veld, compares his own paws with the vast paw prints left by that great beast. Such are my feelings today…"

It has been pointed out that, in the film, Mufasa is killed and Simba flees, pursued by hyenas, only to return to take his rightful place as Lion King and restore the lands to their former glory.

"…I have no arboretum in south Oxfordshire, merely a sort of lopsided laurel. I struggle to run one magazine, whereas Michael told me that at the last count he had 267."

Heseltine was the owner of Haymarket Publishing and his arboretum featured in a BBC Two documentary in 2005.

Johnson said that as Environment Secretary, Hezza liberated many from the captivity of council housing; when Defence Secretary, he stood out against unilateralism under Soviet threat, and in the 1980s helped regenerate Liverpool and the East End of London.

His constituency, Henley, Boris went on, was "like a land of dreams". He said when one stood at the cutting just below the M40's junction 6 – "the Khyber Pass of the Chilterns" – one had the same vision of beauty seen by Thomas Hardy's *Jude The Obscure*. Then there were "the Wittenham Clumps which were famously painted by Constable, and the towers of Didcot power station which were not". Watlington had a first-rate fish-and-chip shop, while the historic village of Ewelme "has the claim to be the centre of English literature and language, as Chaucer's niece is buried there".

There was also had a serious side to his speech. He pointed out the damage foot and mouth had done to the area, and the many rural pubs and post offices that were closing.

"There are pockets of genuine deprivation, problems of poverty and problems of posterity," he said. "For every affluent estate agent in south Oxfordshire – there are quite a few – there are dozens, if not hundreds, of young people who cannot afford housing in the area and whose needs must be attended."

The decline of rural pubs and communities was spurred on by "the punitive measures taken by the police" over drink-driving. So Chancellor Gordon Brown "should offer a tax break to Brakspeare's 2.5 … One can drink three pints of it without coming near exceeding the limit."

Johnson did not often speak in the House – only twice in his first five months. He appeared for around half of the votes and was ranked 525th out of the 659 MPs for attendance. But then, within four months of entering the chamber, on top of his other journalistic commitments, he published *Friends, Voters, Countrymen*. His attendance slipped further in his second term and he rebelled against the Tory whip five times.

Boris was not at home in the House of Commons. He was mercilessly teased for being an Old Etonian, mussing up his hair behind the speaker's chair and having to rush off to put the next edition of the *Spectator* to bed. What's more, the gritty northern Labour MPs on the opposite benches were not his natural audience. Classical references did not impress them; nor did his bumbling Bertie Wooster routine.

"People think I have a bumbling eccentric veneer which hides the fact I am a genius," he said. "I think it is the other way around."

Boris openly admitted his performance in the Commons was "crap".

"I'm not yet world statesman class, frankly," he said. "I've soldiered away on committees, yes, and asked oodles of questions. But they [the sketch writers] don't report them."

Meanwhile, he was at war with the party leadership. He even commissioned Steve Bell to produce a cover showing Michael Portillo pissing on party leader Iain Duncan Smith's head. But IDS needed Boris, who was so popular around the country that he could, by then, command a £25,000 appearance fee. Fan clubs were set up by Home Counties mothers and students at Durham University. He had a greater reach than any other politician. Telling *GQ* magazine why its readers should vote Tory, he said: "Your car will go faster, your girlfriend will have a bigger bra size. It's an attested fact that, under Conservative governments the quality of living of the British people has immeasurably improved, leading to better denticians, higher calcium consumption, leading inexorably to superior mammary development."

Such statements were a ploy he admitted, cloaking a serious intent.

"If you clown around, you may be able to creep up on people with your ideas, and spring them on them unexpectedly," he said.

Unable to discipline Boris, IDS tried to co-opt him. He was to attend the party leader on Wednesday mornings to help him prepare for Prime Minister's Questions. But this failed to curb the wayward Boris. In 2002, the *Spectator* made Tony Blair their Parliamentarian of the Year. He was, Boris said, "the coolest cat in town" – when

Labour benches threaten to rebel, "he quells them as Zeus quelling a bunch of sea-nymphs".

However, his admiration was not unalloyed. He added: "This was a politician who opposed the Falklands war but who has now sent British forces overseas twice on successful engagements."

When chastised for this award by Tory grandees, Boris blamed others on the staff who had given Blair "not the wooden spoon, not the booby prize, but the Top Gong". Nevertheless, Boris was still called in to coach IDS for PMQs, alongside David Cameron and George Osborne who were more committed. Wednesday was press day at the *Spectator* and Boris's attendance began to drop off.

Boris later made amends for the *Spectator* award by writing a column in the *Telegraph* entitled: "Isn't it time to impeach Blair over Iraq?" – even though Boris himself had supported the war. The *Sunday Times* said: "It is impossible to dislike a man who reverses his opinions on a sixpence, declaring with a harrumphing laugh: 'No, it's total bollocks, isn't it? It's balls.'"

Nor did his constituents feel they were getting a "fair squeeze of the sauce bottle", as Boris put it, until, at the Mayor of Henley's annual dinner, he was hit in the face by a bread roll flung by a Labour councillor. The *Henley Standard* rose to his defence and Boris offered to write a column for them, though they, too, had to put up with his cavalier approach to deadlines.

Again, he knew how to woo the punters.

"If Amsterdam or Leningrad vie for the title of Venice of the North," he wrote, "then Venice – what compliment is high enough?

Venice, with all her civilization and ancient beauty, Venice with her addiction to curious aquatic means of transport, yes, my friends, Venice is the Henley of the South."

Boris and his family were soon sought-after guests at Henley garden parties. He also spearheaded local campaigns but, as always, his time-keeping was not up to scratch. On one occasion he failed to turn up at all as he had been test-driving a Ferrari and had run out of petrol in the fast-lane of the A40 in rush hour, causing a massive tailback.

Sometimes, Petronella Wyatt would be sent in his stead; if he did turn up he would often write his speech on the back of a serviette a few moments before he was due to deliver it, just as he had when visiting girls' schools for debating competitions.

As a constituency residence, he first rented a cottage in Swyncombe. Then in 2003, he bought a £650,000 house in Thame that would be big enough for all the family. The tax payer made a generous contribution through MPs' expenses. A large swimming pool was added; the shelves indoors were filled with improving books. However, given her political views, Marina did not take to living in Henley at all.

When Michael Howard replaced Iain Duncan Smith as leader, he made Boris vice-chairman of the Conservative Party. The whips were against this; Boris was always missing votes on the flimsiest of excuses. Nevertheless, he was quickly promoted to Shadow Arts Minister.

Within minutes of accepting the post, he delivered his off-the-cuff plan to save Britain's arts: "Day one, and I have a six-point programme. I haven't cleared this with anybody, but here is what I think. On coming to power I am going to institute a Windows spell check in English so that schoolchildren in this country no longer feel they have got it wrong when they spell words correctly.

"The Greeks are going to be given an indistinguishable replica of all the Parthenon marbles, done in the most beautiful marble dust to end this acrimonious dispute between our great nations.

"I am going to open up the bandwidth, so there is much more freedom on the radio stations. I am going to reduce some of the stuff allocated to the Pentagon, so you can get the Rolling Stones in Oxfordshire. I am fed up with just listening to treacly old Magic.

"Fourth? I can't remember what point four is. Ah, yes. We are going to convene a summit with Damien Hirst and the rest of the gang at which they are going to explain to the nation what it all means. Let us have a national 'mission to explain' by the Saatchi mob, which will be massively popular.

"We're going to have a national poetry Olympiad to restore rhyme and scansion. There will be some sort of stoop of wine for the winning prize.

"Point six is to move away from Labour's grim, utilitarian approach to culture. I took particular exception to [Education Secretary] Charles Clarke's attack on the classics. If we can't study ancient languages, culture and art, we are deracinating ourselves."

As for Estelle Morris MP, the current Minister for the Arts: "She is a charming lady."

Soon after his appointment, the marketing company Superbrands put Boris on their "cool list", alongside Johnny Depp, Bose stereo and Diesel clothes. The company explained: "… being able to zig, when everybody else zags … there isn't anybody else quite like him. And because he's funny."

Chapter Nine – Bonking Boris

With Boris away in the House, sex scandals were breaking out at the *Spectator*, or *Sextator* as it soon became known. Associate editor Rod Liddle was having an affair with the blonde on reception who was half his age. When his wife found out, she told all to the *Daily Mail*. In the article, she accused Boris of running the "whole place like a knocking shop. It was a case of all being lads together, all girls in short skirts, and 'phwooar, good on yer Rod'."

Next it was discovered that the *Spectator*'s publisher Kimberly Quinn was having an affair with Home Secretary David Blunkett. She had also bedded the Spectator's wine correspondent Simon Hoggart.

While Boris's expected promotion to editor of the *Sunday Telegraph* was again put on hold, Conrad Black found himself the subject of an investigation by the US Securities & Exchange Commission. Hollinger, the parent company for both the *Telegraph* and the *Spectator*, sued Black for $200 million over alleged irregularities and he sold out to the Barclay brothers. Instead of sticking up for his mentor, Boris published a scathing attack on Blake and his wife, while mercilessly lampooning him in private.

Boris was still riding high. His novel *Seventy Two Virgins* had just come out and received a good review from Douglas Hurd – in the *Spectator* it must be said. He said: "I guess that he wrote this in three days, flat out." Hurd also noted that the book mocks every possible attitude to the Iraq War – "which seems in harmony with the official *Spectator* line of supporting the war but impeaching the man who started it".

Parallels between Boris and the book's bike-riding protagonist, Roger Barlow MP, were too good to miss. Boris wrote: "To a man like Roger Barlow, the whole world just seemed to be a complicated joke, an accidental jumble of ingredients on the cosmic stove, which produced our selfish genes. For Barlow, everything was always up for grabs, capable of dispute; and religion, laws, principle, custom – these were nothing by sticks we plucked from the wayside to support our faltering steps."

Even so, Boris was still being tipped for the top job, to which he modestly quipped: "My chances of being PM are about as good as the chances of finding Elvis on Mars, or my being reincarnated as an olive."

In New York's *Vanity Fair* magazine, contributing editor Michael Wolff was comparing him to Ronald Reagan and Arnold Schwarzenegger, though "his state of dishevelment is as great as any I've seen in an employed person". It went on to say that he "has achieved near mythic status in the UK … While he may more and more often be mentioned as a future Prime Minister, it is always with incredulity".

But bad luck was right around the corner. Having no time to write a leader, Boris called Simon Heffer and asked him to dash one off. The piece was to be about Liverpool's reaction to the death of Ken

Bigley, a Liverpudlian contractor who had been beheaded by Jihadists in Iraq. The city, it said, was "hooked on grief and likes to wallow in a sense of vicarious victimhood".

It went on: "The extreme reaction to Mr Bigley's murder is fed by the fact that he was a Liverpudlian. A combination of economic misfortune ... and an excessive predilection for welfarism have created a peculiar and deeply unattractive psyche among many Liverpudlians. They see themselves, whenever possible, as victims and resent their victim status, yet at the same time they wallow in it. Part of this flawed psychological state is that they cannot accept that they might have made any contribution to their misfortunes but seek rather to blame someone else for it."

To add insult to injury, it went on to mention the sensitive topic of the Hillsborough disaster, where 96 Liverpool supporters had died.

"The deaths of more than 50 Liverpool football supporters at Hillsborough in 1989 was undeniably a greater tragedy. But that is no excuse for Liverpool's failure to acknowledge the part played in the disaster by drunken fans. The police became a convenient scapegoat, and the *Sun* a whipping boy for daring to hint at the wider causes."

The *Spectator* was first taken to task for downsizing the death toll from 96 to "more than 50" and an independent panel in 2012 concluded that no Liverpool fans were responsible in any way for the disaster, and that its main cause was a "lack of police control".

The leader was not by-lined, so Boris had to carry the can. What made it worse was that Michael Howard had once been a candidate

187

in Liverpool Edge Hill and was a supporter of Liverpool FC. He dismissed the article as "nonsense from beginning to end", and Boris was duly despatched to Liverpool to apologize in what became known as "Operation Scouse Grovel".

In the eye of the storm, Boris was in his element. He insisted that Michael Howard – or just Howard as he insisted on calling him – was "completely wrong to say that the article was 'nonsense from beginning to end'. I don't think he could have read it properly."

Boris was not into damage limitation. While he admitted that the article presented an "outdated stereotype" and apologized for claiming that drunken Liverpool fans contributed to the Hillsborough disaster, he did not retract the broad thrust of the article.

The moment of truth came when Ken Bigley's brother Paul phoned into a radio station Boris was on to tell him: "You are a self-centred, pompous twit – even your body language on TV is wrong. You don't look right, never mind act right. Get out of public life."

When Boris tried to repeat his apology, Paul Bigley cut him off, saying: "You're waffling again."

On his way out of the studio, he was hijacked by Janet Dacombe whose baby son had been harvested for organs without permission at Liverpool's Alder Hey hospital. She, too, demanded an apology.

"Oh well, that's very interesting," said Boris. "I will report back to Michael Howard and he will write to you."

She insisted on a reply that afternoon.

"Are you trying to save your political career?" yelled a journalist.

"I haven't got a political career," replied Boris. At the end of the day, he said: "I feel like a squeezed lemon on the subject."

Otherwise, Boris came through unscathed. Not only did sales of the *Spectator* increase in the city, it boosted his popularity among fans of Manchester United, Liverpool FC's greatest rivals, dubbing them "self-pity city" and chanting: "There's only one Boris Johnson."

Political commentator and Man U fan Michael Crick said: "This was the first and only time a politician had been celebrated in song." He said there were even Boris badges and leaflets at their Old Trafford ground.

In the end Boris felt he had been forgiven by the people of Liverpool, quipping: "The quality of Mersey is not strained."

The furore had only just died down when rumours surfaced that Boris was having an affair with Petronella Wyatt, the Fleet Street femme fatale who had once conspired to ensnare David Cameron. It had been going on for four years and much of it had been conducted through her "Singular Life" column in the *Spectator* for those who could read between the lines. Sometimes, though, her articles carried a womanly rebuke.

"If a man cannot organize his clothes it is often an indication that he cannot organize much else – either his life or the country," she wrote.

It was a cosy relationship. Petronella even came on a family holiday with Marina and the kids, and there was the irresistible detail of the couple circling her St. John's Wood home in a taxi, snogging on the backseat while the driver played a tape of her singing Puccini.

"Boris doesn't tip much," the cabbie complained.

Even the *Telegraph* cast Boris in the role of the dumb blond in this story, while Boris denied everything with characteristic panache.

"It is complete balderdash," he said. "It is an inverted pyramid of piffle. It is all completely untrue and ludicrous conjecture. I am amazed people can write this drivel."

His use of the word "piffle" delighted those sketch writers who remember his middle name was "de Pfeffel". Despite his protestations, Marina kicked him out in the tweed suit he stood up in. He appeared in the same garb in an otherwise formal do – the Spectator's Parliamentarian of the Year lunch at Claridge's. Both Marina and Petronella were no-shows. Which was as well, as the "Boris problem" was on everyone's lips over the Krug champagne.

Sharing the stage with Michael Howard, Boris spoke of "shrugging off the assaults of the press, which can be less than wholly helpful".

Howard then called the *Spectator* "political Viagra".

"Mr Johnson, listening, froze," wrote columnist Quentin Letts. "His eyes, at that moment, were comparable to the stilled headlamps of a prize turbot on some fishmonger's stall. The mouth assumed a fishy quality, too: gaping, rounded, assembled into an expression of hooked horror."

Mr Howard proceeded to tease his underling, at length. He praised the "terrific enthusiasm" with which Mr Johnson undertook his "various duties".

"You were keen to make your mark on the City of Culture" – Liverpool – "And you succeeded beyond my wildest dreams."

Apparently Boris was not enjoying this.

"Outrageous," he muttered.

"Jacques Cousteau, caught several leagues under the sea, could barely have looked shorter of oxygen," Letts continued.

"Keep it up, Boris!" cried Mr Howard to gales of laughter.

"The audience at a Frankie Howerd film could not have been quicker to seize on the nuances of this phrase," Letts concluded.

Soon Boris was patching it up with Marina, believing that he had lived to fight another day, when Petronella Wyatt's mother told the *News of the World* that her daughter had just had an abortion.

"Of course she told Boris in advance. Apparently he agreed with her decision and his reaction was one of immense relief – just like any other married man caught out by his infidelity," she said.

In the tabloids, "bumbling Boris" and "boisterous Boris" had become "bonking Boris".

Despite being caught out in a lie, Boris refused to quit as Shadow Arts Minister or party vice-chairman. He argued that it was not only justifiable but positively desirable to lie about one's sexual life – citing President Clinton's denial of having sex with Monica Lewinsky.

Michael Howard did not take this view and promptly sacked him. Boris reacted by having a stiff drink, then seizing the opportunity to write about the "surreal joy of being sacked" in the *Telegraph*.

191

"Nothing excites compassion, in friend and foe alike, as much as the sight of you ker-splonked on the Tarmac with your propeller buried six feet under," he wrote, concluding: "My friends, as I have discovered myself, there are no disasters, only opportunities. And, indeed, opportunities for fresh disasters."

Sympathy over his sacking won Marina around. Their marriage was on the mend and he was soon caught in floral short and skull-and-crossbones ski-hat out on his early morning run from their Islington home – though he returned to find the front door locked and had to wait to be let in.

Despite his long career in journalism, he was less than sanguine about the predations of the paparazzi.

"I saw the bloody photographers outside, so I jumped over the garden wall at the back and eluded them. Then I totally forgot they were there on the way back," he said, When asked why didn't he climb over the wall again rather than stand, locked out, by his front door, he said: "You know when you go for a run, you get rather elated. I sort of had this idea that I would mow them down, like a scene in an old Sylvester Stallone film."

But Boris was not about to mend his ways. In the midst of the storm, he overcame a rare bout of flu and went to speak at an Oxford Union debate at the invitation of Ruzwana Bashir with whom, the press noted, he enjoyed a "close relationship". There were others. Sonia Purnell calls one chapter of her biography, *Just Boris*, "Busting with Spunk", a phase said to have emanated from the lips of the rotund Lothario himself. Elsewhere he boasted of being fuelled by "weapons-grade testosterone".

Nevertheless womenfolk rushed to his aid. Margaret Cook, jilted wife of Foreign Secretary Robin Cook, compared the charms of the Marina's jumpers and Petronella's décolletage. She also pointed out that Marina had ousted Allegra with the age-old ploy of falling pregnant. Even the housewives of Henley on Thames put the blame on Marina – for going out to work.

Male friends warned that, wed to a ferocious lawyer, he might be in for ruinous divorce. Other's blamed Petronella's mother for encouraging her daughter to bag Boris after DC had escaped her grasps. At the *Telegraph* though, editor Charles Moore indulged his star columnist, saying: "I told Boris I don't care about what he does in his private life and he told me, 'Nor do I.'"

Dan Colson also entered in the spirit of the thing, saying: "He always looked like he had just got out of bed and, apparently, he had."

Nobody blamed Boris – least of all Boris. But politically, he had paid the price, though even Michael Howard was soon having second thoughts.

Under the high-minded Catholic Barclay Brothers, things were set to change at the *Spectator*. They installed as chief executive Andrew Neil, who told the BBC: "I think the more time the editor spends in Doughty Street editing the magazine and the less we see of him in the newspapers, then the better for the editor and the better for the magazine."

Ping pong in the garden was banned, along with Ann Sindall's Jack Russell and, presumably, daytime sex.

However, the soap-opera goings-on had only boosted sales of the *Spectator*. Boris was charging £10,000 a time for after-dinner speaking and earning £150,000 a year from TV and other journalism. This was on top of his £59,000 MP's salary and the undisclosed sum he got for editing the *Spectator*. He could even have afforded a new suit.

Neil promised a "period of quiet" at the *Spectator*. Instead, the BBC aired the *Spectator Affair*, a behind-the-scenes look at the workings of the magazine. Fearing that he would be asked about his personal life, Boris, at first, avoided appearing. Then, when it seemed that others were co-operating, he deigned to give an on-camera interview.

His inquisitor said: "I have never seen anyone who is tougher behind the eyes than him in a billion years of interviewing … He is a charmingly evasive ruthless customer."

Though the peccadillos of Rod Liddle and Kimberly Quinn were given an airing, Petronella was airbrushed – leading to accusations that Boris had done a deal over access with the producers.

Conrad Black appeared, saying: "Boris had his charms, but Boris is not Mr Loyalty."

Behind closed doors, Boris blamed Black for his downfall. However, they made it up and Boris wrote a supportive letter to the judge in Chicago when Black came to trial.

When it came to the election in 2005, Boris was kept in check – even though he was potentially a vote winner. His one contribution to the campaign was an update of his old *GQ* joke, which was now rendered: "Voting Tory will cause your wife to have bigger breasts and increase your chances of owning a BMW M3."

The only place he was to be seen was in Teignbridge, South Devon, where Stanley was a candidate. He lost out to the Lib-Dems. The Conservatives barely put a dent in Labour's stranglehold on parliament, but Boris increased his majority in Henley, though he was nowhere to be seen.

After that, he withdrew from constituency politics. He had bigger concerns in town. *Spectator* staffers Lloyd Evans and Toby Young put on the play *Who's the Daddy?* at the King's Head Theatre in Islington, satirizing the bonkathon at the magazine. Other staffers packed the audience.

"I don't know whether I'll have time to catch it before it closes," Boris told the press. "I'm certainly issuing no instructions to staff about it. It will not be deemed an act of disloyalty to go and see it."

The authors had warned him of its content. He replied, resignedly: "I always had a feeling that my life would turn into a farce."

They even borrowed this line for the play where Boris's character says: "Fine – turn my life into a farce, everyone else has."

Questioned about the play in the *Independent*, he said he felt "eirenic" – peace-seeking – and "ataraxic" – serenely calm.

"I was due for a good kicking," he admitted.

He could have sacked Evans and Young, but showed them the indulgence others had shown him. In response, they turned down the offer of a transfer to the West End.

Marina stood by him, turning out for the annual *Spectator* summer party. But Boris said any day he expected to join the "Valhalla of ex-*Spectator* editors". Meanwhile the atmosphere at the office had become one of "monastic seclusion and contemplation".

"I can't quite remember what happens in *The Name of the Rose*," he said. "Oh, it gets rather racy, doesn't it? OK, forget it."

Chapter Ten – Eton Rules

After losing the 2005 election, Michael Howard stepped down as Tory leader. Asked whether he would stand for the position, Boris said: "My hat is firmly in the sock draw, where it will remain."

Instead he supported fellow OE David Cameron against the "Stain" David Davis, who then was favourite.

"I'm backing David Cameron's campaign out of pure, cynical self-interest," Boris said. With his backing, Cameron's odds shortened considerably.

Cameron won the leadership. Nevertheless, Boris plainly thought the job was rightfully his and, in his *Telegraph* column, damned Cameron with faint praise.

"Over the past few months I have lost count of the number of people who have asked me – satirically – why I am not standing in the current Tory leadership contest; and after I have bumbled out some reply, they have always said, oh well, who are you backing? 'David Cameron,' I have said, quick as a flash, and for the most part this answer has so far drawn a look of anxious blankness, the look you see when people are sure that they ought to have read some classic work, and are in two minds whether to bluff it out or admit ignorance. 'Oh yes,' they say, mentally noting that they ought to get to grips with the subject of David Cameron, along with Stephen

Hawking's *Brief History of Time* and *Midnight's Children* by Salman Rushdie ..."

Though Boris was a supporter, he said: "You may not want to go quite as far as Bruce Anderson, whose essay on Cameron in this week's *Spectator* is a kind of tear-sodden *nunc dimittis*. Like old Simeon in the temple, Brucie has seen our salvation ... though you may not be prepared to agree with him that Cameron is our saviour and a light to lighten the gentiles, and the glory of the Tory party ..."

What's more Cameron was a young whipper-snapper. But the forty-one-year-old Boris conceded "it has been the 38-year-old's week".

The problem was that Cameron was just a pale imitation of the real deal.

"... I like this stuff about there being a 'we as well as a me' in politics. I like his constant repetition of 'we're all in this together'; indeed, I am vain enough to have a feeling that he nicked it from me."

He concluded: "... the Tories must rediscover compassionate Conservative ... That is the job for Cameron, and Cameron is the man for the job." A neat phrase, perhaps, but it sounds like empty sloganeering.

Boris had yet to choose between journalism and politics. On *Desert Island Discs*, Sue Lawley pushed him on the point. He flannelled, but was forced to come down on the side of politics. Then she got him to pitch for a job on David Cameron's front bench. What of his own ambitions for leadership? she went on. Boris had to admit: "I suppose all politicians in the end are like crazed wasps in a jam jar, each individually convinced they are going to make it … My silicon chip, my ambition silicon chip, has been programmed to try to scrabble my way up this *curus honorum*, this ladder of things …"

Like most other people, Boris had spent years writing and revising his list of eight records. In the event, when he handed over his selection, the producer sucked her teeth.

"Your choices … it's just that they seem so political," she said. "It's like you're kind of trying to appeal to everyone, a bit of Stones, a bit of Bach, you know. I mean, Nigella Lawson chose Eminem!"

His other choices were the Beatles, Van Morrison, Hadyn, The Clash, Beethoven and the theme tune from *Test Match Special*.

"I was shattered, and insulted to the core," Boris wrote in the *New Statesman*. "'But I love this music. And, much as I like him, I don't want Eminem on a desert island.' She then tried to reassure me about my taste, and what exquisite choices they were, but I couldn't help feeling, as she left, that I had failed one of life's great tests."

With a nod from Boris, Frank Johnson wrote an imaginary conversion between David Cameron and George Osborne which was published in the *Spectator*.

Mr Cameron: 'Anything else we need worry about, George?'

Mr Osborne: 'Well, yeah. Boris has just announced on Desert Island Discs that he's going into politics.'

Mr Cameron: 'What? Why isn't he content to be MP for Henley?'

Mr Osborne: 'He said he thought it will soon be time for him to choose. So if we win, he says he'd like to be a front-bench spokesman for agriculture or trade or something like that.'

Mr Cameron: 'You mean, he intends to join our front bench?'

Mr Osborne: 'Looks like it. What are we gonna do?'

Mr Cameron: 'Well, I shall say that I think he has taken a brave and correct decision in the interests of country and party, and that I wish him well in whatever he turns his considerable talents to next, and that none of this is any reflection on his ability.'

Mr Osborne: 'No, Dave. That's what you say when he has to resign from the front bench again, not when he joins it again.'

Mr Cameron: 'Oh, yes. I was jumping ahead a bit.'

As it was, when Cameron announced his Shadow Cabinet, Boris wasn't in it. The next day, he was appointed Shadow Minister for Higher Education and he was forced to give up the editorship of the *Spectator*. Cameron was not about to risk another Liverpool.

Instead, Boris gave him a Portsmouth, calling it a city "too full of drugs, obesity, underachievement and Labour MPs". Then he managed to offend a whole country, saying the Tory party had "become used to Papua New Guinea-style orgies of cannibalism and chief-killing". When the High Commissioner demanded an apology, Boris said: "Add Papua New Guinea to my global itinerary of apologies."

At the *Times Higher Education Supplement*, political correspondent Anna Fazakerley greeted his appointment with glee. "Rumple and ready to rumble" the headline said. However, Boris stepped back from his early promise to slash "looney degrees in windsurfing at Bangor University". He now said: "My instincts are not to go around trying to exterminate Mickey Mouse courses. One man's Mickey Mouse course is another's *literae humanitores*."

Bolstered by his stand in higher education, Boris stood for the position of rector of Edinburgh University – a position previously held by Gladstone, Gordon Brown and his hero Churchill. This gave him an opportunity to chat up students in short skirts and he got to sign one student's bare chest. However, there was an "Anyone But Boris" campaign with the slogan "Practice safe X – don't wake up with a dumb blond".

In the vote, he came third to a Green member of the Scottish Parliament and the editor of the *Scotsman*, a fellow OE.

Relieved of his duties at the *Spectator*, Boris found time hanging heavy on his hands, so he made a two part series for BBC Two called *Dream of Rome*. In it, he sought to discover how the ancient Romans managed to run a united empire, while the European Union could not.

He wrote a book to accompany the series and was heard complaining "bloody hard work, this book thing". Asked how long it had taken him, he replied: "Bloody hell, two weeks."

In anyone else's hands this might have been dull, but to Boris the Barbarians were "clad in nothing but the kind of fur accessories you might find in a fetish shop – a seal-skin jockstrap, a rabbit-skin loincloth" and their wives would "bare their breasts in a kind of *Sun* Page 3 exhortation to the troops".

He made a follow-up TV series called *After Rome*: *Holy War and Conquest*. This got him into trouble with the parliamentary authorities as he had not declared his shareholding in the production company. He also upped his fee for his weekly column on the *Telegraph* and was bringing in over half-a-million pounds a year.

The topic for his column would come from a session with his parliamentary staff. Then a staffer would do the research. This did not take long as Boris insisted there should be no more than three facts per article. Then he would knock the whole thing out in ninety minutes. For each column he got £5,000.

He would also encourage staffers compete to come up with topics that would cause the most catastrophic consequences for his career, such as "Why I believe in a European superstate". Boris's favourite was "Why David Cameron is a complete c**t". He even got round to writing the intro.

His opinions were never less than forthright. Interviewed for the Christian magazine *Third Way*, he expressed pride in his "mongrel" background and his Muslim, Jewish and Christian heritage. Indeed, his children were a quarter Indian. And he told Muslim students that they should inter-marry – "then all our problems would go away".

After less than four months in office, Bonking Boris was at it again. This time, the *News of the World* caught him sneaking in and out of Anna Fazackerley's Chelsea flat. They may have been discussing higher education, but why was Boris so furtive and why did he find it necessary to cover his distinctive hair with a beanie hat? They were seen out together and one source said: "They also got overheated in the back of a cab and were told to 'cool it' by the driver taking them to a function."

On one occasion, after two hours with Anna, the *News of the World* said Boris emerged sheepishly and took a taxi to Petronella's place in St John's Wood where he stayed for another couple of hours before returning home to Marina.

When the paper approached Boris to give them a quote, he said: "You're very kind. But no thank you. Absolutely not. No comment whatsoever. Thanks a lot. Bye."

As a result of the article, Anna had to duck out of covering his fact-finding tour of China. While he was away, Marina lodged a protest with the Press Complaints Commission when journalists besieged their Islington home. She moved her wedding ring to her middle figure and the children were farmed out to a friend in the country. But after Boris returned from China, he took Marina away on a family holiday and the press coverage died down.

Cameron took no action, while on his website, Boris said: "Heads down and tin hats on while news stories fly." His secretary added: "Boris's talent and ability can weather any storm."

Certainly being branded a philanderer in the tabloids had not dented his popularity. When he was asked to play in a charity football match against Germany, the crowd cried: "We want Boris."

He took his higher-education brief very seriously, visiting universities around the country – though often turning up in impossibly flashy cars, courtesy of his *GQ* motoring column. He would be in his parliamentary office until nine or ten at night, writing speeches and would often work over the weekends. There were, as always, the prolonged absences though, and his boss, Shadow Education Secretary David Willetts, found it difficult to work with a junior who had a higher political profile that his.

Boris managed to upstage Cameron's first Conservative Party Conference speech in 2006, by taking a swipe at Jamie Oliver who was promoting healthy eating in schools. At a fringe meeting Boris stood up for mothers who smuggled fast food to the children through school fences.

"I say let people eat what they like," he said. "Why shouldn't they push pies through the railings? If I was in charge, I would get rid of Jamie Oliver."

To still the maelstrom, Boris was forced to back down, saying: "I was completely misquoted. Jamie Oliver is a saint," later calling him "the Messiah".

Putting a brave face on it, Cameron said: "It's been a great week – even Boris made it until Tuesday afternoon before he put his foot in it."

While critics were saying that Boris could not be taken seriously, they suddenly took him very seriously when he said in the *Telegraph* that Iran should be assisted to build an atomic bomb – which it would eventually build anyway – in return for assurances that it would not attack Israel and make progress towards democracy. It was a line he had pushed early. It was rumoured that Boris's planned elevation to Shadow Minister for Europe was scuppered by this piece. Boris, it was concluded, was still more interested in journalism than politics.

Further humiliation came when Michael Gove, one of Boris's stooges at Oxford and three years his junior, was installed as his boss. The entire Shadow Cabinet was now younger than him.

At the time, the Tories were having difficulties finding a candidate to stand for Mayor of London against Labour's incumbent Ken Livingstone. At one point, they had even discussed fielding a joint Conservative-Lib Dem candidate in Greg Dyke, but he pulled out.

Polling data indicated that Livingstone could be defeated and Veronica Wadley, editor the London *Evening Standard*, let it be known that she would support Boris. Denied advancement inside parliament, Boris realized that the only way he could make it to the top was to establish a power base outside it.

News that he intended to stand was leaked in bumbling fashion by Boris, by accident, when he bumped in to the BBC political editor Nick Robinson, who he had known at university, on the tube. But neither Robinson – nor any of the people he told – believed it was true.

Boris then denied that he was going to stand. Then he admitted that being Mayor of London was a "fantastic job" and that a lot of people were urging him to run, but he did not want to give up his Henley constituency, along with his parliamentary salary and expenses.

A compromise was reached. This allowed him to keep his constituency until the mayoral election. But he gave up his Shadow Higher Education brief immediately and got his nomination in for

Mayor just hours before the deadline. The party leadership still had cold feet, but they had no other credible candidate.

Boris outside parliament was not under their control. On the other hand, with his flair for publicity, he did not need their endorsement. Boris romped through the newly instituted primaries. Then came the main event – Boris versus Ken.

Livingstone admitted that Boris was the most formidable opponent he had faced, but that being Mayor was not a job for a celebrity. Running a huge city was a serious business. Ken had a good track record in the job, modernizing transport and, on his watch, London had overtaken New York as the world's financial centre. Against that Boris had a rocky parliamentary career and a couple of sex scandals to his name.

What's more, Gordon Brown had just taken over as Prime Minister and Labour were having a honeymoon. Boris also had a millstone. In twenty years of journalism, he had committed his thoughts to paper. With a skilled set of scissors, it was possible to make him look like a racist, a homophobe, a right-wing bigot and a toff totally out of touch with the needs of a modern multicultural city like London. Ken was a Londoner, born and bred, while Boris had no natural affinity for the city.

Nevertheless with The Clash blaring out "London Calling", Boris launched his campaign. His one policy announcement was the abolition of the bendy bus and the return of the sturdy double-decker. While he was serious about becoming Mayor, he said, he reserved the right to make jokes.

"Are you too funny to be Mayor?" asked a reporter from the *Wall Street Journal*.

He was a hero to the party faithful at the Conservative conference that year, though the governor of California's comments had him dubbed "The Fumbulator" on the internet. Still, the publicity did him no harm.

The Conservative Party's position was strengthened when Brown "bottled it" that summer and decided not to go for an early election. This was a relief for Boris who would have fought in Henley again as well as running for Mayor. He had enough on his plate. On top of his constituency work, there were still his weekly column for the *Telegraph*, his television commitments and a new book to promote. Many assumed that he was not actually out to win mayoralty, believing that a credible defeat would give his political standing enough of a boost.

He had a small campaign team ensconced in Centre Point over a mile-and-a-half from Tory headquarters in Millbank Tower. They had little experience and were up against Livingstone's Labour Party machine that outnumbered them by thirty to one. Boris depended on his fame and charisma to do the job.

The Tory top brass lent him some staff, but it was soon clear that his campaign was a shambles. It was only then that the Conservatives realised that, if they could not take London, it would harm their chances in the next general election.

Boris, as always, got lucky. In the *Evening Standard*, Andrew Gilligan accused Lee Jasper, Livingstone's director of policing and equalities, of cronyism and corruption. He was later cleared, but the story tarnished the reputation of the Labour regime.

The campaign headquarters was moved to the old County Hall building across the river from parliament, so Boris could be reined in, and the former treasurer of the Conservative Party Lord Marland was sent in with a war chest of £1.5 million.

Next Lynton Crosby, the "Wizard of Oz" who had won four elections of John Howard in Australia, was brought in. He did not come cheap. When Crosby and Marland invited him to lunch, Boris knew what was coming. He first thing he told them was that he had already booked an appointment for a haircut. They told him that losing was not an option and if he let them down – "we'll cut your fucking knees off".

Another Australian, James McGrath, was called in to apply military discipline. With his hair cut and combed, Boris was kitted out with smart suits, shirts and ties. A third antipodean was employed to give Boris media training. His bumbling may have been all right on *Have I Got News For You?* but now he need to speak in sound bites.

Although Boris found his minders "scary", research had shown them that Boris had a likeability factor that eclipsed the other candidates, even with people who did not share his political opinions. While Livingstone was a leftist ideologue inhabiting Zone One and Two, Boris was somehow apolitical, speaking up for the concerns of ordinary Londoners rather than playing politics. Boris's team targeted the outer suburbs where people were more likely to vote Tory, but had not voted in previous mayoral elections. In response, Labour wheeled out its political big guns. But the more they demonized Boris as "some sort of right-wing Neanderthal", the better he looked. No one could be as bad as they said.

Crosby then made Boris "green", despite his previous assaults on the tree-hugging brigade. This was a rerun of his campaign to be president of the Oxford Union – he would be everything to everyone.

Boris was still widely perceived as clueless, while Livingstone had been in office for eight years. But Ken was past his sell-by date and BoJo, as he was then dubbed, was seen as the coming man.

Then Marina put her shoulder to the wheel, going on walkabouts with Boris, sometimes with David and Samantha Cameron. She was a well-known leftie and her appearance by his side made it seem that even she had been won over.

In the first televised debate with Ken and the Lib-Dem candidate Brian Paddick, Boris got the better of it by raising the recent spate of teenage murders.

"It breaks my heart to see so many kids growing up scared, and so many adults scared of kids," he said. No sign of the joking, bumbling Boris of old there.

When Labour Home Secretary Jacqui Smith said that she was frightened to go out for a kebab in her area of Peckham, Boris declared: "I want London to be safe for Jacqui Smith … I want the most dangerous thing in Peckham to be the kebab itself."

Crime became Boris's lead policy of the campaign – on the journalistic grounds that "if it bleeds, it leads," Livingstone said.

However, abolishing the bendy buses came back to bite Boris. He said that the cost of employing conductors on the fleet of new Routemasters would be just £8 million a year. It would be more, as more Routemasters would be needed.

Boris was soon said to be "fuming" that the police were pursuing him for the theft of Tariq Aziz's cigar case, which Boris had taken from the bombed-out ruins of Saddam Hussein's Deputy Prime Minister's home. He had admitted as much in his *Telegraph* column five years earlier. He was forced to hand it over four months later, but by then he was Mayor of London.

At the time, he protested that Scotland Yard should be concentrating on knife crime, rather than harassing him over a little souvenir collecting. As luck would have it, the matter was eclipsed by fresh allegations of sleaze against Lee Jasper – this time that he was having an undeclared relationship with a woman who received funding from City Hall. He was forced to resign, though the police found that there was no criminal case to answer.

With Livingstone on the back foot, Boris attacked the overseas offices – or Kenbassies – he had set up and the "ludicrous Pyonyang-style newspaper" City Hall produced. *The Times* then discovered that Livingstone was planning to extend the congestion-charge zone. Boris went on the offensive in the areas concerned, dubbing Ken Livingstone "Ken Leaving-soon". A disastrous budget then caused Labour to slump in the polls.

GQ demonstrated its loyalty by ranking Boris the fourteenth worst dressed British male; Ken came in at number eleven. *The Times* then carried the story that while Gordon Brown had all but written off Livingstone's chances, allies were consoling themselves that a victory for Boris "would be a disaster" for Cameron. To counter this, Cameron turned out alongside Boris at a meeting in Edmonton with black youth leader Ray Lewis, now a regular companion of Boris on the campaign trail.

Boris was, Cameron said, "a man who is as big a figure as Ken Livingstone – and twice as charismatic; a man who is just as determined as Ken Livingstone – and twice as energetic ... I don't always agree with him but I respect the fact that he's absolutely his own man. He's a proper Conservative."

Labour's deputy leader Harriet Harman gave Boris's crime agenda another unwitting boost when she donned a stab-proof vest for a tour of her Peckham constituency with the police. However, he was not helped when the BNP endorsed him on their website. Several black City Hall workers told the *Voice* that they were genuinely afraid of what would happen to them if Boris was elected. But Boris was not the monster portrayed by Livingstone's campaign. People saw that for themselves because of his appearances on *Have I Got News For You?* However, Boris's campaign team had similar worries, fearing that the *Evening Standard*'s unrelenting support might prove counterproductive.

Boris's sexual history did not count against him either when it came out that Ken had five children with three different women. This was not secret, merely private, Ken said: "I don't think anybody in this city is shocked about what consenting adults do."

So nothing was made of "Bonking Boris" during the campaign. On this matter, the two men called a gentlemanly truce. However, there were some ructions when *Marie Claire* published an interview where Boris admitted to smoking dope before going up to Oxford and saying that he might have taken cocaine while he was there.

Labour ministers and MPs were banned from calling Boris by his first name. He was to be called "Boris Johnson" or "the Conservative candidate". "Boris" made him sound too cuddly. So Boris stopped referring to Livingstone as "Ken", calling him rather "the Labour mayor".

Former Tory MP George Walden urged Londoners not to vote, saying of Boris: "… the most entertaining thing about Johnson is when he puts on his serious, solicitous look. Like David Cameron, he is coming to believe in his own sincerity. Servility to celebrity has partially replaced class deference, and the adoring polls suggest that Johnson benefits from both. A Greek grocer I knew put his finger on it. Musing about how Alan Clark imagined relieving himself on the public from his ministerial balcony, he concluded: 'The English don't mind being pissed on, so long as it's from a great height.'"

While Boris had backtracked from the £8 million for conductors on Routemasters, he was skewered by Jeremy Paxman on *Newsnight* who asked him thirteen times for a more realistic figure. Later he was caught privately admitting that the figure would be closer to £100 million. But being slapped down by Paxman somehow made Boris all the more endearing and, in the TV debates, even Ken was seen to laugh at his jokes.

At a public meeting in Westminster, Boris broke with the party line and called for an amnesty for illegal immigrants. This sank accusations that he was a racist once and for all. With his Turkish heritage and quarter-Indian children, Boris told the interviewer on the BBC Asian Network: "You can't out-ethnic me."

At a meeting of the gay-rights lobby Stonewall, he was asked whether he could "out-gay the gays" by revealing whether, perhaps at Eton, he had had some gay sexual experience. After a pause, Boris said: "Er ... not so far."

Asked on the *Politics Show* to sum up the other two candidates in one word, Brian Paddick said: "Tragedy; comedy."

With a week to go, Cameron's advisors were already discussing how to protect their leader should anything go wrong when Boris was in office. Boris was already telling the viewers of *Question Time*: "I would gladly embarrass any government that is in power, if it was in the interests of Londoners."

While Ken was practically conceding defeat in the press, Boris's friends were still wielding the knife. On the eve of polling, Simon Heffer wrote in the *Telegraph*: "Mr Johnson is not a politician. He is an act ... The act is calculated and it has required serious application and timing of the sort of which only a clever man is capable. For some of us the joke has worn not thin, but out ... It conceals two things: a blinding lack of attention to detail, and (though this might seem to sit ill with the first point) a ruthless ambition ... The guiding theme of his life is the charm of doing nothing properly. His sins themselves are charming in that they are the sort of failings that upset the Edwardians, and few others since. He is pushy, he is thoughtless, he is indiscreet about his private life. None of this matters much to anyone these days, which is why he has gone so far in spite of them, and tomorrow may go further still."

On the morning of the poll itself, the *Guardian* ran five pages of blistering personal attacks on Boris, under the headline: "Be Afraid, Be Very Afraid."

The following day, their worst nightmare came true.

Chapter Eleven – Boss Boris

More than a million people had voted for Boris, giving him a fifty-thousand lead over Ken on the first count. When the second preference votes were counted, Boris's lead increased to 140,000. Ken said that Boris bounced over to him and said: "This is all Gordon Brown's fault."

Boris's success astounded even him. He was the first Conservative to hold executive power in eleven years and he had the biggest personal mandate of any politician in the country, the third biggest in Europe behind the presidents of Russia and France.

He made a gracious acceptance speech without a hint of triumphalism, thanking particularly Ken Livingstone for shaping the office of Mayor and his service to London. Echoing Mrs Thatcher's quoting of St Francis of Assisi, he said: "We have a new team ready to go into City Hall. Where there have been mistakes we will rectify them. Where there are achievements we will build on them. Where there are neglected opportunities we will seize on them … Let's get cracking tomorrow and let's have a drink tonight."

Later, he aped Tony Blair's New Labour pledge with: "I was elected as new Boris and I will govern as new Boris."

Then it was off to Millbank Tower where they were entertained by an all-girl blonde band and Cameron, awkwardly, held Boris's hand aloft as the winner. Cameron later quipped that Boris would not let go – it was "like the first gay marriage".

The following day he attended the signing-in ceremony in a plain dark suit and white shirt, where four hundred supporters chanted: "Bor-ris! Bor-ris!" He then tripped over and complained that the stage had been booby-trapped. Afterwards, he warned any dogs in the manger that he would have them humanely euthanized.

He would take over the seals of office the following day.

"Until that time," he said. "I imagine there are shredding machines quietly puffing and panting away in various parts of the building, and quite right too. Heaven knows what we shall uncover in the course of the next few days."

When he took over at City Hall, Boris shook the hands of the six-hundred staff. Unlike Ken, he did not bring a team with him and only slowly began making his own appointments. Ann Sindall was brought in from the *Spectator*. Guto Harri, a friend from Oxford, became director of communications, having previously turned down a similar post with Cameron. Ray Lewis became Deputy Mayor for Young People.

Cameron loyalist Nick Boles was installed as acting chief of staff by Central Office, leading Boris to suspect he was a spy. Indeed, he reported back that Boris seemed ill-prepared for office. Meanwhile Rachel went on *Question Time* and promised Londoner's years of "Boris-induced sunshine". His victory, she said, had given the Tory party "a collective orgasm".

A week after becoming mayor, Boris bade farewell to his parliamentary constituency with a letter to the *Henley Standard* that read: "When I set out on my mission to unseat Ken Livingstone more than nine months ago, there were all kinds of risks. There was a considerable risk that I would be thrashed by the Great Newt. And then there was a risk that I would win – and therefore lose Henley, just about the loveliest seat in the House of Commons. At the time, I have to admit, it seemed a pretty small risk…"

It was clear to some that Boris did not even want the mayoralty. He told Brian Paddick that he was "very concerned he was going to win because of the money". The salary, at £143,911, was more than the Prime Minister's, but he had around £100,000 a year in school fees to pay. He feared that he would have to give up his column on the *Telegraph*, but the paper found him too valuable to let go. To deflect criticism, Boles insisted that he donate a fifth of his fee to charity.

"It's outrageous," he said. "I've been raped."

Nevertheless he had to concede the "Boles tax". However, he managed to trim the twenty percent down to around seven. It would be used to support students of journalism and pay for Classics courses in state schools.

Senior editors at the *Telegraph* were assigned to baby-sit his column and steer him away from any potentially explosive topics, though Boris feared this might quench his natural exuberance. Even so, disregarding copyright, he would also publish his columns on his own website before they came out in the paper, often giving him extra coverage in the media.

Boris basked in his new stardom, doing the round of social events. The *Tatler* said: "The priapic Bozza is pure party Viagra."

He even made up with the *Guardian*, telling them: "Every day I wake up in a state of wonderment that I have been elected – obviously knowing that millions of other people wake up in a state of wonderment that I have been elected too."

There were the pitfalls of office to deal with too. Ray Lewis had to go when it was discovered that his CV was not all he said it was and James McGrath, who had worked on Boris's campaign countering accusations of racism, was summarily fired after he said something that could have been interpreted as racist.

When it was clear that Boris, on his own admission, did not "have the faintest clue" what he was doing, Simon Milton, leader of Westminster Council, was called into play the Stuart Reid role. Alongside him would be Tim Parker, whose job-slashing in industry had earned him the nickname "the Prince of Darkness". But when it was clear that Boris could not just be a figurehead as he planned, Parker had to go too.

To demonstrate his political virility, Boris took a swing at Cameron in the *Telegraph*, saying that Britain's sporting triumphs at the Beijing Olympics show that it was "piffle" to claim that we had a "broken society" as the party leader had said. Then Boris set off to wave the flag at the closing ceremony in Beijing looking like a human laundry basket.

Among the old staffers at City Hall, few heads rolled. They were not a bunch of Marxists as Boris had been told and most were happy to stay on. One of their few complaints was that Boris did not take a shower after cycling to work and the windows of City Hall – which Boris dubbed "the testicle" – were not designed to open. Deodorant was recommended.

Boris set about ousting Metropolitan Police Commissioner Sir Ian Blair, who was still embroiled in the fallout from the shooting of Jean Charles de Menezes. Though he did not actually have the power to sack him, Boris assumed the role of Brutus. Blair resigned, saying: "Without the Mayor's backing I do not think I can continue." Policing continued to cause problems throughout his administration, but after the departure of Blair, Boris judiciously stepped down as chairman of the Metropolitan Police Authority.

After a year in office, a poll in the *Evening Standard* gave Boris a ringing endorsement. The *Economist* said: "It may be that a bold personality and cautious policies are the right mix for a London mayor."

He suffered little criticism in the press as he had worked alongside most of the editors. Even Jeremy Paxman was a family friend. What's more, he could take credit for Crossrail and the preparations for the 2012 Olympics both set in motion during Ken Livingstone's watch. The only criticism that hit home was that Boris was now boring. Nevertheless, *Time* magazine named him one of the world's hundred most influential people – a list devoid of the name Cameron, who Boris continued to snipe at tangentially from the columns of the *Telegraph*.

Boris found that he was well out of the House of Commons when the expenses scandal struck in May 2009. David Cameron had to pay back nearly £1,000 after charging for having wisteria removed from a chimney, while Gordon Brown had to repay £12,400. Boris claimed to be amazed at the expense claims of his former colleagues.

"I'm almost embarrassed that I seem to have completely failed to claim for all these things that my colleagues claimed," he said. "Unless you're completely insane or devious or a Liberal Democrat, then there is no way you can fiddle your bike expenses."

As it was the *Telegraph* who was spilling the beans of MPs' expenses, he was on the inside track. It turned out that he claimed – legitimately – £85,299 for mortgage payments on his constituency home, plus £16.50 for a Remembrance Sunday wreath. This had been an oversight, he said, which he happily repaid.

However, as the net spread wider, a deputy mayor was caught fiddling his expenses. Bicycling Boris himself had run up a bill of £4,698 in taxis during his first year in office.

"Where exactly does Boris cycle?" asked one blogger. "Is it just to and from photo shoots?"

At the time, Boris was being photographed a lot on his bike when the tube drivers went out on strike. Boris and his bike became a symbol of Londoners carrying on regardless.

Becoming mayor had not hurt Boris's earning power as he had feared. The family moved into a £2.3-million Georgian townhouse overlooking Regent's Canal. In contravention of planning regulations, he erected a shed on the back balcony. The local council made him take it down. When LBC's Nick Ferrari asked him about it, Boris accused him of "intruding in the private grief" of a man now sadly "ex-shed".

On the trip to New York to visit Mayor Michael Bloomberg, Boris found Americans lining up in Times Square to shake his hand. Back in London, he took a cameo role in *EastEnders*, playing himself, though he has never seen the show – or, for that matter, *Coronation Street*.

At the party conference in the run-up to the 2010 General Election, Boris managed to upstage both David Cameron and William Hague, playing the well-worn Eurosceptic card and wooing the crowd with the line: "It's wonderful to be here in Manchester – one of the few great British cities I have yet to insult."

Cameron was furious.

Boris went on to stick up for bankers. They had, after all, backed his mayoral campaign.

As mayor, the Tory party could not hold him under its thrall. He treated House of Commons committees with contempt and Mayor's Question Time in front of the twenty-five members of the London Assembly as a game. He would dodge questions and hurl carefully crafted insults at his inquisitors.

Chapter Twelve – Call for Boris

When the general election was called in 2010, Boris predicted a majority of forty for David Cameron. He stepped in to help his brother Jo, who was running in Orpington, and generously donated a few *bon mots*. He called Gordon Brown a "holepunch-hurling horror" and Nick Clegg "a cutprice edition of David Cameron hastily knocked off by a Shanghai sweatshop to satisfy unexpected market demand".

When Cameron failed to win a majority, Rachel Johnson tweeted: "It's all gone tits up. Time to call for Boris."

In the end though, with the help of Nick Clegg, Cameron took the keys to Number Ten. This changed everything for Boris. In his skilfully crafted plan, he had intended only to serve one term as mayor, then return to Westminster as the party's saviour.

While Boris pondered his future, news broke that City Hall art adviser Helen Macintyre had a blonde-haired child. She was a brunette. So was her long-term partner, Canadian financier Pierre Rolin, who Macintyre had persuaded to pay £80,000 towards Boris's "Olympian Erection" – the 400-foot red metal ArcelorMittal Orbit tower at the Olympic Park. Soon after, she moved out of his £5-million property. Boris neither confirmed nor denied that the child was his.

A source close to Johnson said: "It's quite likely he hasn't the faintest idea."

Rolin was not invited to the Olympic games. Nor did he get his money back.

Once more Marina removed her wedding ring and threw him out of the house. And once again she took him back again. Everything was patched up with a two-week family holiday in Tanzania, though Boris got swept away by the strong current in the Zanzibar Channel and had to be rescued. After another trip, to India, he was allowed to return home.

The resort they stayed at cost over £700 a night. This was in the age of Osborne austerity. Boris got away with even this without comment.

Osborne tried to clip his wings by slashing London's budget. Boris thwarted this by leaping to the defence of Crossrail, though he knew it was not under threat. On another occasion, when negotiating new powers for the mayor, Boris launched himself over the table to grab Cameron's briefing papers, resulting in an unseemly tug of war.

Before he had left office, Ken Livingstone had suggested a scheme of street-corner bike hire across the city. These became Boris bikes and he was happy to take credit for them at the 2012 election. "Borismaster" buses hit the streets and, the champion of small government, committed public money to build a cable car over the river between the Royal Docks at the O2 Arena. He also backed the building of "Boris Island" in the Thames Estuary to house a new international airport.

When the government proposed a £400-a-week cap on housing benefit, which would force poorer people out of central London, Boris went on air and said: "What we will not accept is any kind of Kosovo-style social cleansing of London."

And he continued to use his *Telegraph* column and appearances on *Question Time* to take pot shots at Cameron's policies. Perhaps not wanting him back in the House of Commons, Cameron invited Boris and Marina to dinner at Number Ten, letting it be known that he was four-square behind Boris's re-election as mayor. Once again he would take on Ken.

When the phone-hacking scandal broke, Boris hastily cancelled a family outing to a Take That concert as guests of Rebekah Brooks and let Cameron take the flak.

During the riots of 2011, Boris was in a Winnebago in the Rockies with Marina and the kids. Boris did not return. This bore a poor comparison to Ken Livingstone who flew back on the first plane from Singapore, where he was lobbying for the Olympics, after the 7/7 bombings in 2005.

But when Theresa May and David Cameron broke off their holidays, Boris's hand was forced to catch a flight home. Beating them to the punch, he filed a piece for the *Evening Standard* on the way. Nevertheless, in riot-torn areas, he was greeted with jeers.

Then suddenly, he was seen with a broom, ready to lead the clean-up of the streets, and the jeers turned to cheers. He dined with David Cameron that night. The following morning, on the *Today* programme, he blamed the riots on the government for cutting police numbers.

Boris then turned up thirty minutes late for a meeting of COBRA, the national emergency committee. Cameron was incandescent.

He was in trouble again when Sir Michael Scholar, chairman of the UK Statistics Authority said that Boris had given misleading figures to the House of Commons Home Affairs Select Committee. Boris dismissed Scholar as a "Labour stooge".

Boris claimed that serious youth crime was coming down, when in fact stabbings were going up, and that police numbers were going up, when in the Metropolitan area they were going down. However, he scored highly in the law-and-order debate in 2009, intervening personally in a mugging when documentary film maker and Ken Livingstone supporter Franny Armstrong was pushed against a car by a group of young girls, one wielding an iron bar. Boris, who was cycling past, picked up the iron bar and cycled after the girls calling them "oiks". Armstrong described Boris as her "knight on a shining bicycle".

London's budget was in difficulties – not least because of the money spent on buying land for the Olympics – but that did not stop Boris pumping money into the outer borough that had won him the election in 2008. Trailing Ken in the black vote, he posed with Pauline Pearce, who had famously ticked off the rioters in Hackney. In the *Telegraph*, the picture carried the headline: "Heroine backs Boris." However, she told the *Guardian*: "I didn't say I am backing Boris."

Boris failed to sparkle at that year's party conference, after Cameron introduced him with the line: "I don't know a four-letter word to describe him."

Ken Clarke had said ministers had been recording audio books for the blind. Speculating over the battle to succeed him, Cameron quipped that George Osborne "went straight for *The Man Who Would Be King*. I'm afraid Boris missed out. Instead he chose *The Joy of ... Sss ... Cycling*."

While Paxman gave him an easy ride, when he returned to the capital, Boris was greeted with a poster campaign by a dating agency that specialized in discrete encounters for the married. It featured a huge picture of Boris and carried the caption: "Affairs now guaranteed – no matter what you look like."

The Occupy London protesters were camped outside St Paul's Cathedral. One of their banners read: "Boris loves bankers." His response was to call on judges to have the "cojones" to kick the "crusties" out. He then claimed to be a crusty himself.

"It's an affectionate term from one crusty to another," he said, "and I wish them a Merry Crustmas." He also pointed out that their protest had not yet triggered the resignation of a single banker – while "three blameless clerics" had been "felled".

When Ken won approval with a promise to cut fares, Boris promised: "What I will not do is play politics with fares." Then when George Osborne stumped up £130 million, he did a quick U-turn.

He also came under criticism for his £4-million-a-mile cycling superhighways, which appeared to be nothing more than a line of blue paint that did nothing to protect their users. Indeed, two people died at one junction in 2011.

Though Boris's record in office was arguably thin, *GQ* hailed him "the most influential man in Britain". As Prime Minister, Cameron came in second. Another problem Boris had in the mayoral race was the speculation that he would run for parliament in the 2015 general election, which was a full year before his tenure of City Hall would run out. Boris told the BBC that there was "not a snowball's chance in Hades" that he would stand.

"I don't think I will do another big job in politics," he said.

The job of mayor was enough for him, though he found time to write *Johnson's Life of London*, which was soon recognized as a leadership manifesto. Meanwhile, he was ridiculing Cameron and Osborne's stance on the Euro crisis and even offering an alternative policy. Ken Livingstone joked that, in the mayoral election, he knew he could count on the vote of at least one Tory – the mayor himself.

Despite Boris's evident reluctance to spend another four years in City Hall, he won the election, albeit with a reduced majority. Two months later, the London Olympics gave him an international stage. He made a splash when he was left dangling from zip wire over Victoria Park waving Union Jacks.

Boris continued being what critics called a part-time mayor, writing his column for the *Telegraph*, though the £250,000 a year he got for it he told the BBC's *Hardtalk* was "chicken feed". In

February 2013, he was thrown out of a meeting of the London Assembly after calling the members "great supine protoplasmic invertebrate jellies". He pushed ahead with his plan to close down ticket offices on the Underground, providing an automated ticketing system instead, and promised a twenty-four-hour service at the weekends.

By March 2014, Boris's snowball seems to have survived its sojourn in Hell and he was looking for a London seat. In July, Sir John Randall, MP for the safe Conservative seat of Uxbridge and South Ruislip, said he would not be running in the general election. Boris was adopted as candidate there in September. The following month, he published his book *The Churchill Factor*. People drew their own conclusions.

By January 2015, with the election still four months away, the *Sunday Times* was reporting that Boris Johnson would be offered a cabinet post immediately if the Conservatives won – possibly a minister without portfolio until his term as mayor ran out.

Boris invited George Osborne over for lunch in his old constituency home near Thame. Afterwards they took a walk in the fields where they thrashed out a "peace pact" – Osborne would leave the way clear for Johnson to take on Theresa May for the leadership if Cameron was forced out.

The *Sunday Times* called this the "Thame cottage accord" and compared it to the Granita deal where Gordon Brown agreed to defer to Tony Blair over dinner at an Islington restaurant.

So, while Boris might not succeed in his ambition to become "world king", the leadership of the Conservative Party and, possibly, the premiership were within his grasp. Being President of the United States would have to wait a little longer.

Nevertheless, Boris prepared for his role as world statesman in typical fashion by calling ISIS jihadis a bunch of porn-watching "wankers" who turn to violence because they "are not making it with girls…"

Meanwhile Boris awaits the call.

Alan Johnson

Left Standing

Introduction

In the middle of November 2014, with less than six months to go before a general election, leader of the opposition Ed Miliband scored the worst poll rating of any party leader since records began. Miliband shrugged and said: "What does not kill you makes you stronger."

According to *The Times*, the remark acknowledged that an attempted coup involving a number of Labour frontbenchers to top Miliband and install Alan Johnson in his place had failed. This was partly because Johnson had already refused the job. Only the day before, he had announced that he would never pitch for the leadership.

"I have never stood for the leadership of my party – and for the avoidance of doubt, regardless of the circumstances, I never will," he said. "Ed Miliband will lead us into an election that I am convinced we can win. It was my decision to walk away from frontline politics, not Ed's. The position of Labour leader has been vacated twice during my time as a member of parliament. Both times I chose not to stand. I happen to think that a better person took this onerous role on each occasion."

But some still had their doubts. Politicians have been known to change their minds. Some even back, apparently unwillingly, into the limelight. However reluctant to take the top job, they can usually be persuaded that the party – or even the country – needs them.

Alan Johnson is eminently qualified for the role as party leader. Elected to parliament in 1997, he has served as Home Secretary, Health Secretary, Education Secretary and Shadow Chancellor of the Exchequer. By contrast, Ed Miliband entered parliament in 2005 and served in the lesser government posts of Minister for the Cabinet Office, Chancellor of the Duchy of Lancaster and Secretary of State for Energy and Climate Change, before he was elected leader of the Labour Party.

Miliband is a committed Brownite, having worked as an advisor in the Treasury before joining Brown's cabinet. Johnson has served in government under both Blair and Brown.

The two men could not be more different. Miliband is a North London intellectual. His father, a Belgian-born Jew of Polish origin, was a Marxist academic. Ed and his brother David learnt their politics over the dinner table in Primrose Hill, then Ed went on to study at Oxford, the London School of Economics and Harvard. Johnson was born in Notting Hill, now the gentrified home of some Tory grandees, but then a slum, riven by race riots in the 1960s. He left school at fifteen, became a postman and worked his way up through the Union of Communication Workers to become its General Secretary, before becoming an MP.

Alan Johnson is old-school Labour with a genuine working-class background. He supported David Miliband in his bid to become leader of the Labour Party after the resignation of Gordon Brown.

After serving just three-and-a-half months as Ed Miliband's Shadow Chancellor, he resigned for personal reasons.

Since then, he has declined Ed's offers to return to the Shadow Cabinet. Asked if he would consider a role in the Cabinet if Miliband won the 2015 election, he said: "I would be more interested, but I am not gagging for it."

No matter what he says, many politicians and pundits regard him as the Labour leader – or even Prime Minister – in waiting.

Nigel Cawthorne

Bloomsbury, December 2014

www.nigel-cawthorne.com

Chapter One – The Wilds of West London

Alan Johnson was born on 17 May 1950 in Paddington General Hospital. His father, Steven Arthur Johnson, was a lance corporal in the British Army when he married Lilian May Gibson at Kensington Registry Office in January 1945. It was a low-key affair with, it appears, a single witness. The Registry Office was still swathed in barbed wire as a wartime precaution.

The bride – and later Alan's mother – Lily had been born in Liverpool in May 1921, the second of a family of ten, two of whom had died from pneumonia after contracting measles. Lily's grandmother had died at the age of forty-two. Her mother also perished at that age from cervical cancer.

By then the Gibsons had moved to a semi-detached house in a new council estate in Anfield. It had three bedrooms, a bathroom with an inside lavatory, electricity and gardens front and back. For a working-class family in the 1920s, this was heaven.

Nevertheless, for Lily, there were difficulties. While her mother was giving birth to her younger siblings, she was expected to help run the household. A clever girl, she was also supposed to be studying for a scholarship. Then, in the increasingly overcrowded conditions, she contracted rheumatic fever which damaged her heart. It also led to her being hospitalized with St. Virus Dance, the involuntary jerking of the limbs. The only cure, then, was to be strapped to the bed frame which rattled with her spasms. As a result, she was berated by the other patients who were trying to sleep.

Despite these trials, she won her scholarship, but could not take up her place when her father refused to pay for her school uniform. Forced to leave school early, she took a job in the Co-op. Then, during the war, she had joined the NAAFI – the Navy, Army and Air Force Institutes that provided recreational facilities for enlisted men – and left Liverpool for good.

While little over five feet tall, Lily had grown to be a ravishing red head. She got engaged to an older man who had contracted tuberculosis and died. On the rebound, she was waiting to be demobbed when she met Alan's father at dance in 1944.

Steve was a musician. He told Lily that he had been offered a job by the big band leader Bert Ambrose, but turned him down as Steve refused to learn to read music. Self-taught, he played the piano entirely by ear. A natural showman, he wore a pair of white gloves when he played in the NAAFI and had a reputation as a ladies' man.

Lily should have known better, but the war was ending and everyone was fired with optimism. Steve was a Londoner and that is where they would make their home. But as a scouser Lily was made to feel like an outsider in Notting Hill and remained self-conscious about her Liverpool accent for the rest of her life.

After the war, Steve looked for work as a painter and decorator, but he was feckless and could not hold down a job for long. Instead he supported his habits of drinking, gambling and smoking by playing the piano at parties, weddings and, in the evenings and at Sunday lunchtimes, around local pubs.

Their first child, Linda, came along in 1947. This was before the foundation of the National Health Service the following year. Linda was just 5lbs 4oz at birth, while Alan, who came along two years after the establishment of the NHS, was a healthy 10lbs. But, at birth, his umbilical cord was twisted around his neck. The difficult birth took its toll on Lily's already fragile health. Afterwards, as it would have been dangerous for her to have any more children, she was sterilized.

The baby boy was christened Alan, after the 1940s' film star Alan Ladd, and he was given the middle name Arthur, after his father. The family were then living in one room in a housing trust property in Southam Street, next to the railway lines at the back of Paddington Station. The slums there had been condemned fifteen years earlier but not even the Luftwaffe had knocked them down.

When Alan came along, the family moved into two rooms on an upper floor. They used one room as a bedroom, the other as a living room. There was no electricity. Lighting was provided by gas mantles – or, more often than not due to their poverty, tiny makeshift candles that were little more than a blob of wax with a wick in it. The gas was provided by putting a shilling in the meter.

In the evening, a lamplighter would arrive on his bike to light the streetlights outside the communal front door. There was a single squalid lavatory in the backyard with newspaper torn into squares as lavatory paper and a cistern that froze in the winter. Rather than use the lavatory on cold dark nights, they kept a bucket in the bedroom. Consequently, the tiny flat stank of urine – or worse. Washing was done in the sink, though clothes were sent out to the "bagwash" when they could afford it.

Before the gentrification of Notting Hill Gate, the area was officially designated North Kensington, but known locally as Kensal Town – or just The Town. Since the 1980s, estate agents have expanded the boundaries of Notting Hill and former dilapidated properties have been spruced up and sold to incoming middle-class families. Well served by the underground, the area is handy for Westminster and the City.

Alan's father boozed and gambled most of his money away. He contributed little to the household budget. So despite her poor health, Lily took jobs as a cleaner and a general dogsbody in the well-to-do houses of South Kensington and Ladbroke Grove. Her pay barely covered the rent and the meagre meals that she scraped together for the children. Food was in short supply generally. Rationing was still in force until Alan was four. Their staple diet was bread, butter and eggs, though sometimes there was nothing to eat but bread and dripping. At best, living was hand to mouth. Johnson remembered spending his childhood in an almost constant state of gnawing hunger. As a result, when Steve came home well-nourished and drunk, there would be a row that would sometimes end in violence.

In winter, Lily would scavenge coal for the fire. The children would sleep under mountains of old clothes for warmth. Conditions were little better in the summer. As the coal fire had to be used for cooking and hot water, it remained lit even on the hottest summer's day. They had no fridge to put food in. Milk had to be kept cool by standing it in a bowl of water and butter consigned to the coolest corner of the pantry, which was nothing more than a tiny cupboard on an outside wall, ventilated by an air-brick. As a result, the place was infested with flies, cockroaches, earwigs, beetles and all kinds of other insects.

Like Lily, Steve had not been brought up in such squalor. Alan recalled being taken by his father to visit his Nanny Johnson who lived with her youngest son, Uncle Jim, in Delgano Gardens. She had a flat in one of the blocks provided by the trust established by the American philanthropist George Peabody. Light and breezy, it was free of bugs, damp and the smell of decay. It had an indoor lavatory, a bath in the kitchen and even a carpet in the front room, along with a comfy sofa. Alan particularly remembered going there as a toddler because his father had held his hand. It was the only time he could remember them having physical contact – at least of a tender sort.

As post-war austerity lifted, Steve got an office job. Like most working-class men of that era, Steve turned out in an immaculately clean suit on a Sunday. It had been pressed with a flat-iron heated on the fire and his shoes had been polished and shined. While he headed off on his own, Lily would take the two children to play on what they called the The Debry – a bombsite remaining from the Blitz. Much of the area was filled rubble. There were other dangers. The railing around the recesses that allowed light into basements had been removed to make armaments. Instead they were fenced off ineffectively with sheets of corrugated iron.

On a Sunday, Steve would go and play the piano in the pub, before returning home for his Sunday dinner. Back then, the pubs were only open at a lunchtime on a Sunday from 12 until 2 pm. They would close all afternoon, open again at 7, and close at 10.30. The shops, too, were closed on a Sunday, though costermongers laden with shellfish, and a man with a horse and cart with a huge barrel of vinegar on the back toured the streets. As well as a condiment for the cockles and whelks, vinegar was used as a cure-all for cuts and bruises.

While Lily believed in God, they did not go to church on a Sunday. Nevertheless there were some observances at home. For example, it was considered sinful to play cards on the Sabbath. Beyond the teachings of the Church of England, Lily had a profound belief in astrology – not that the predictions she found *Old Moore's Almanack*, the monthly horoscope magazine *Prediction* or the *Daily Sketch* ever seemed to do her any good. None of this made any sense to Alan, who was an unshakeable atheist from an early age.

The children would go out either with their father or their mother – never the two together. Sometimes Steve would take them to visit his friends Ted and Elsie. Their children were of a similar age and Alan and Linda would play with them in the yard behind the flats. One day when Ted, a lorry driver, was away, Linda returned to the flat and walked in to find Steve in bed with Elsie.

When Lily discovered what had been going on, there was a huge row. This was overheard by the children and most of the neighbourhood. Steve then went to live with Elsie. When he returned home six months later, Elsie was pregnant and returned to Ted, who agreed to bring up Alan's half-brother David as his own. However, when Steve did not keep up the child-support payments he had promised, Ted came round and knocked him to the ground.

Despite everything, Lily took Steve back. It was important back then that children were seen to have two parents. Apparently, she still loved Steve and hoped he would change. In an attempt to make a fresh start, she arranged a family holiday in Liverpool, the first time Lily had returned there since the war.

They went by coach, with the kids kitted out in new clothes provided by loans from the Provident. But this only added to the burden of debt Lily had accumulated by getting things on tick at local stores.

Lily's mother was long dead and she did not get on with her father who was a martinet, but the trip was an opportunity for her to get together with her brothers and sisters, and their spouses. Steve managed to spoil the atmosphere by flirting with her sisters, upsetting both them and their husbands, and while Lily took the children around the places she had known as a child and to the seaside at New Brighton, Steve returned to his old ways, spending most of his time away from the family in the local boozers. The reconciliation was a failure.

Back in London, Steve spent more time away from home, disappearing for weekends to the seaside or taking time to travel down to Kent to play the piano for the hop-pickers. Still, little of the money he earned came into the household and Lily continued struggling to make ends meet. The children were dressed in second-hand clothes from the street market in Portobello Road and there was little food on the table. Only rarely would there be enough money left for the kids to get sixpence pocket money on Saturday.

Things got a little better when Alan started school at Wornington Road Infants' where he and Linda qualified for free school meals. Supremely conscious of the value of a good education, Lily had enrolled the two children at the local library. By the time they started school, both of them could already read.

When Alan was six, the family was moved down the street to a ramshackle apartment where they had three rooms and a gas cooker on the landing. This provided much needed heat in the winter. There were few cars on the roads in those days and kids could play in the street. Given the cramped accommodation and the state of the sanitation, adults and children alike preferred to spend a lot of the time outdoors, whatever the weather. However, before the Clear Air Acts of 1956 and 1960, they had to contend with the pea-souper fogs, which were actually smogs cause by the smoke from coal fires. It was dangerous to breathe the air and everything was covered in a thin layer of grim. Even so, Lily and other housewives spent hours scrubbing their front steps, turning them gleaming white in the gathering gloom.

While the building they had moved to was just as damp and dilapidated as the one they had left, Alan and Linda now had their own bedroom which they shared. It was on a landing also occupied by another family. The new place had electricity provided, like the gas, by a coin-operated meter. Despite these improvements, there was no heating in the bedroom, so before bedtime Lily would pop an earthenware hot-water bottle into the bed to warm the linen sheets. Otherwise the room, particularly the lino floor, was freezing. It was not unusual in those days to find frost on the inside of the window panes.

Lily's dream came true when the family was offered a council house. But it was out in the new town being built at Crawley in Sussex thirty miles to the south and Steve refused to move out of Notting Hill.

If the children managed to save up sixpence, they would head for the pie-and-mash shop or the sweet shops where they would buy homemade fizzy pop. Another favourite was the German bakers. They could not afford to buy anything there, but would nourish themselves on the smell of fresh-baked doughnuts and bread.

In those days, almost all adults smoked. Steve rolled his own, while Lily cut her factory-rolled cigarettes in half with an old razor blade, but still she would smoke them with the panache of a movie star.

Once a week, she would doll herself up, doing her hair and putting on her make-up in a broken mirror, and go to the pictures. Linda would be left in charge of her younger brother. When Lily returned, she would tell them of what she had seen on the silver screen. Though this was Lily's one indulgence, Steve resented the few pennies she spent on the cinema, though, on the rare occasions he backed a winner, the family saw none of the proceeds. Until 1960, off-course betting was illegal in the UK. Nevertheless Steve sent the children to place his bets with a nearby bookmaker, though they were never trusted to collect his winnings, if there were any.

Sometimes Steve would take the children with him when he was playing the piano at a wedding. This was a treat. They were particularly proud of him when he played at the children's Christmas party held in nearby Westbourne Grove. There they got Christmas presents, usually a book, which they treasured.

Otherwise Steve spent most of the day in bed and, though there was a decrepit piano in the flat, he made no effort to teach his children to play. Indeed, he kept it locked. They were also denied access to the music he kept on his collection of old shellac 78s as they had no record player. The only entertainment at home came from a radio that Lily rented.

Like the rest of the adult population of Britain in the 1950s, Steve and Lily did the pools and listened intently to the football results being read out on the wireless at five o'clock on a Saturday afternoon. In 1957, Lily won £90, the equivalent of £2,000 today. She used the money to make down payments on furniture and treats for the kids. Soon she was unable to keep up the payments and the kids spent much of their childhood dodging the tallyman. Eventually, most of what she had bought had to be returned.

However, they managed to retain a small, portable Dansette record player and an acoustic guitar, which Alan was determined to master. Though they could not afford to buy any new records, they could at least listen to Steve's old 78s.

Chapter Two – Family Break-up

By her early thirties, Lily was already prematurely middle-aged. Though her posh employers still gave her expensive hand-me-downs, she rarely appeared without her floral over-all and headscarf that were then the uniform of the charlady. Despite their poor diet, she had filled out and her face was lined and careworn.

Her doctors recommended rest, but she could not afford to give up her char work. As a result of overwork, she spent the Christmas of 1957 in hospital. On Christmas Eve, Steve disappeared and failed to return. On Christmas Day, alone and abandoned, the children found the Christmas hamper Lily had saved up for. After stuffing themselves with sweets, they decided to cook the chicken they found in it. Stuffing the gas meter with a few precious coins, they lit the oven and put the chicken in. However, they had not realized that they were supposed to unwrap the chicken first. The plastic wrapping melted, giving off acrid fumes and rendering the meat inedible. Further catastrophe was averted by the young Irishwoman who lived in the next landing and came running to the rescue.

After feeding themselves the best they could with the vegetables they had cooked, they set off to walk to Paddington General Hospital. Steve was waiting outside and warned them not to tell their mother that he had not come home – otherwise, she would get upset and die, he said. For the half-hour visiting time, they kept by the pretence that the three of them had had a nice Christmas dinner together. Afterwards, Steve did not come home with them. He did not return for another two days.

Lily was eventually sent home with orders to rest, but within a few weeks she had picked up fresh charring jobs. While she cleaned and scrubbed, the children were left to play in Kensington Gardens with sandwiches wrapped in waxed paper from sliced loaves. They had strict instructions not to talk to strangers and to take shelter in one of the museums on Exhibition Road if it rained. The Victoria and Albert Museum, the Science Museum and, particularly, the Natural History Museum became regular haunts.

Alan and Linda were only left to their own devices out of necessity. Otherwise, Lily bought them up with a firm hand. She was not against giving them a slap. They ran errands for neighbours and were commended for their manners.

While Lily's marriage had plainly been a disaster, she was determined to stick at it. A stigma was still attached to separation and divorce. But the children were conscious that there was something wrong with their parents' relationship, particularly compared with those of the parents of friends.

One particular friend was Tony Cox. He and Alan had met at Wornington Road Infants' School and moved on to Bevington Primary together. Tony's father Albert, in Alan's eyes, was an outstanding example of a decent, hardworking man, who looked after his wife and family and still wore his army beret with pride as a memento of his wartime service in the Royal Engineers. In peacetime, he worked as an engineer on the London Underground, while his wife worked in a fish-and-chip shop in Shepherd's Bush.

In the Coxes' home in Latimer Road, Alan experienced unimaginable luxury. It was warm and clean and they had a whole room where they neither ate nor slept. The whole family had a cooked breakfast every morning and their diet was supplemented with vegetables grown on Albert's allotment. He was a provider. What's more, they had a bookcase that contained a collection of second-hand classics, along with an *Encyclopaedia Britannica*. But, like Steve's piano, it was kept under lock and key. Unlike Alan and Linda, neither Tony nor his sister Carole were interested in reading. Despite repeated hints, Alan was denied access to this treasure trove too.

One interest Alan and Tony shared was collecting the cards that came with sweets, cigarettes and packets of tea. They were swapped or competed for in the playground. This was strictly segregated, with the girls confining their activities to skipping and innocent games involving bouncing balls. Only Linda stood out as something of a tomboy. She was allowed out with her skipping rope to play in the road, while Alan played with his model cowboys and Indians at home.

There were dangers for boys on the streets. At the age of six, Alan had his treasured collection of bus tickets stolen by an older boy. There were fights outside pubs and gangs of toughs roamed the streets. Steve tried to teach Alan to box to defend himself, and although Lily tried to protect him, Alan ended up black and blue.

Steve never used corporal punishments to discipline the young Alan, but he was beaten regularly at school. That was the norm back then.

While Lily liked to keep Alan safe at home, he was allowed out in the company of Tony Cox, who had a spare bike which he lent Alan – until he ran into a young woman coming out of a shop. Tony was also accomplished with his fist, while Alan sought to avert any fight by affecting to look tough. Neither that, nor Tony's fighting ability, were any good when Alan was seized in a headlock by a man in his twenties who was clearly deranged. Tony and their companion Dereck Tapper, the son of one of the recent West Indian immigrants to the neighbourhood, could do nothing as the youth threatened to slice Alan's face open with a piece of glass. Nevertheless, they stood by him until he could make his escape.

At the time, Notting Hill was notorious for the slum-landlord Peter Rachman. He packed West Indians – who were otherwise denied rooms by the offensive and ubiquitous sign that read: "No Blacks, No Irish, No Dogs" – into the overcrowded and inadequate accommodation, charging them extortionate rents. The immigrants also had to suffer the predations of the local Teddy Boys. Once Lily had to give refuge to one young white woman who had the temerity to go out with one of the black men.

In August 1958, an argument between a white woman and her Jamaican husband sparked a full-scale race riot that lasted six days. Over 140 people were arrested with nine white youths given exemplary sentences of five years in jail and fines of £500.

The Notting Hill riots were part of the young Alan's political education. Oswald Mosley, leader of the British Union of Fascists in the 1930s, returned to the streets there as part of the "Keep Britain White" campaign. Lily had no time for him. Her one political icon was Emmeline Pankhurst, founder of the suffragettes.

Nine months after the riots, she tried to intervene when a young black man was murdered by a white gang. Lily knew the man who delivered the fatal blow, but she did not give his name to the police, fearing retaliation. By then she had enough troubles of her own.

Tension grew at home when Linda passed her eleven-plus, which would allow her to go to a grammar school rather than the fearful local Sir Isaac Newton Secondary Modern. As a reward, Lily bought her a dog from Battersea Dogs' Home. Steve refused to have it in the house. When he was there, it had to be chained up in the back yard, whatever the weather.

On one freezing day, he came home unexpectedly – and far from sober – to find the dog in the house. In the ensuing fight, Linda attacked him with a knife, before running off with the dog. She was found hours later out on the open spaces of Wormwood Scrubs. Even Lily realized that this marked the end of any pretence of family life.

Much later in life, Linda revealed her untold suffering at that the hands of their father.

"He had been sexually abusing me since I was about four years old," she said. "It began one Sunday morning when I hopped into bed with mum and dad. Mum got up to make a cup of tea and Alan was asleep in his cot. That was how it started. He would say it was because he loved me."

She was also outspoken about Alan's suffering at the hands of his abusive father.

"Alan was often the victim of Dad's drunken rages," she said. "Dad would pretend he was boxing with him, but the punches were real and hard. He told Alan he was a wimp and he should toughen up and learn to fight, punching as he spoke. Alan was always very brave and would try to fight back but would sometimes cry, which would make me so angry. Then Mum would intervene and get a wallop, too."

At the time, Australia was keen to attract fresh immigrants from the UK and were offering passage for £10. Lily suggested to the kids that the three of them should seek a better life down under. But while Alan and Linda were keen to escape from their father, they were adamant they were not leaving London.

Soon after, Steve walked out. Lily and the children came home one Saturday afternoon to find his meagre possessions and battered suitcase were gone. Alan was just eight years old. He and his older sister were ecstatic. But Lily sat down and wept.

The following day, she went to the pub where Steve played on Sunday lunchtime. There was no sign of him. His family also closed ranks. Lily was blamed for not having been a better wife to him and none of them would tell her where he was. After a while, gossip reached her that Steve had gone to live with Vera, the barmaid he had spent the previous Christmas with. No one knew where. Or so they said.

Finally, Southam Street was scheduled for demolition and Lily and the children were rehoused in Walmer Road, nearer Wormwood Scrubs and Shepherd's Bush. By then Alan was nine and Linda twelve, so the housing trust gave them a four-room flat so that the kids could have separate bedrooms. It also had a kitchen and Lily persuaded the trust to install a bathroom in the a squalid basement, though hot water for the bath still had to be heated on a gas ring. But money was tight and, on the rare occasions they had a bath, they had to share the water. They still had to share an outside lavatory with everyone else in the building. This one had no light.

Despite being rehoused, Lily's mood did not lift and Alan and Linda would hear her sobbing at night. For the children, this was almost as bad as the rows and fights they had overheard when Steve was still with them. She found some comfort when Linda moved into her bedroom with her. This allowed her bedroom to be turned into a living room, complete with a three-piece suite from the Salvation Army, where she could entertain her new friends from Fulham County Grammar School.

Despite the doctors' advice, Lily continued cleaning. She also took a job in a tobacco kiosk, then a café, further supplementing her income doing piece work varnishing wooden toys at home. Soon there was enough coming in to rent a television. Nevertheless, groceries still had to be bought on tick. When further credit was denied, Linda volunteered to work in the shop until the bill was paid off.

Lily decided that she wanted a divorce, so that if Steve could be tracked down, he would be liable to pay her maintenance. But first she had to find him. Meanwhile she returned to hospital for another long stay. Her heart condition, it seemed, was getting worse.

Then her luck changed. Thinking she was alone in one of the flats she cleaned in Notting Hill, she broke down crying. One of the young tenants overheard her and persuaded her to tell him what was wrong. It turned out that he was a journalist and offered to track Steve down for her. He took the simple expedient of phoning the pub where Vera had used to work, saying that he worked for an insurance company and had some money for her. He then visited the address in Dulwich he had been given for her and confirmed that Steve was living there.

The journalist's brother, who also lived in the flat, was a solicitor who, pro bono, obtained a divorce for her, along with a maintenance order for £6 10 shillings a week. A postal order for that amount began arriving every Friday, though payments soon tailed off. This curtailed such treats as fish and chips, and their diet largely returned to potatoes roasted in dripping, bubble and squeak and other left overs. Sometimes they were reduced to eating breakfast cereal twice a day, or bread floating in beef stock.

Nevertheless, with the advent of the 1960s, the family were seized by the new mood of optimism. Linda was doing well at school. Now it was time for Alan to sit his eleven-plus – his mother had ambitions for him to become a draughtsman. It was regular indoor work and you got to wear a suit.

For young Alan, though, there were distractions. Apart from cubs and an attempt to learn to swim that left him with a lifelong fear of water, there were the attractions of a fellow pupil named Linda Kirby. But all attempts to win her affections failed embarrassingly.

Where Alan did excel was his knowledge of the hit parade. Even his music teacher was impressed and, while money was still coming in from Steve, Alan and Linda even bought the latest 45s. Lily encouraged them. They saw Lonnie Donegan in pantomime at the Chiswick Empire and Cliff Richard and the Shadows at the London Palladium. She also bought Alan a crystal set so he could listen to Radio Luxembourg. Even at the age of six or seven, he was writing his own songs and was learning to play the guitar with Bert Weedon's instruction manual *Play in a Day*. His musical ability was the one thing he ascribed to his inheritance from his father.

Alan's other passion was football. He was a Queen's Park Ranger's fan, another thing he inherited from Steve though his father never took him to a match or even talked about football with him. However, he had left behind the QPR handbook from 1947-48, the season they had been promoted, which Alan repeatedly re-read. Lily gave him the money to go to Loftus Road, along with Tony Cox and his father Albert. She later paid for his subscription to *Charles Buchan's Football Monthly*.

He was also a fan of Enid Blyton's Famous Five and the cowboy book *Shane* and became so besotted with the novel's tall, dark hero that he was sorely disappointed when he saw the 1953 film version, starring his short, blond namesake Alan Ladd.

With Tony Cox and other friends, Alan played football and cricket in the streets of Kensal Town. Sometimes they explored the exotic reaches of Kensington Gardens and Holland Park, when peacocks roamed free. Otherwise there was a blasted heath of Wormwood Scrubs with its glowering prison to the west.

The rumour was that there had once been an army camp there. In their fertile – if rather confused – imaginations, British prisoners of war had been held there and tortured by the Japanese. One night, five of them set out to investigate. Among the bunkers, they found a tunnel. It was down there, they believed, that British troops had been incinerated in ovens by their merciless captors. With some trepidation, they entered, believing they were the first to have explored the death camp.

That expedition marked the end of childhood. This fearless band of brothers was about to be broken up by the education system that then sought to separate the sheep from the goats at the age of eleven.

Chapter Three – Big School

Alan Johnson passed his eleven-plus, but others failed and were sent to the dreaded Sir Isaac Newton Secondary Modern. While well-heeled parents were happy to see their children go to the new-style comprehensive in Holland Park, Lily was determined that Alan should go to a grammar school. That, she believed, was the way out of the life of limited opportunities to which she had been consigned.

The nearest grammar school did not even offer him an interview. Another, over the river in Battersea, looked down their nose at him. However, he did get into the Sloane School in Chelsea, along with Tony Cox and Dereck Tapper. This was perhaps due to the progressive views of its veteran headmaster or, more likely, Johnson thinks, because there was a shortage of pupils in the area as the denizens of Chelsea prefer to send their offspring to public schools.

Lily managed to buy a second-hand uniform. Social Services supplied his shoes and, along with free school meals, he was given free travel as the school was more than three miles away.

Johnson hated Sloane Grammar School. It was an enduring embarrassment to be picked out as one of the kids entitled to free school meals. Worse, the school was just five hundred yards from Stamford Bridge and most of the boys were Chelsea supporters.

Tony Cox flourished there. Despite the overt racism of the day, even Dereck Tapper excelled, going head to head in the gym with

Malcolm Macdonald who went on to play football for England. Dereck went on to university and acted at college.

Johnson was more bookish, watching documentaries in the geography block during break time and beginning a life-long love of the work of P.G. Wodehouse. He joined the school choir and sung the school productions of operas.

With her growing children becoming less of a burden, Lily also sought to make a new life for herself. At the behest of the brothers who had organized her divorce, she looked through ads in the lonely-hearts column of the local paper. She met one of the respondents in a nearby pub and, the following week, invited him home. It was vital, the children were told, that they made a good impression on him.

After Steve had left, Lily had taken a screwdriver to the lock on the piano. When her new beau arrived, he regaled them with robust renderings of popular hymns. The kids responded with a cappella versions of show tunes. He then recommended Alan try out for the choir at Westminster Cathedral, revealing that he was a Catholic. That was the last Lily saw of him.

Linda continued working at the local grocery store. She was now bringing regular money into the household and took charge when Lily made increasingly frequent sojourns in hospital.

Trouble ensued when Linda started seeing boys. Lily tried to impose strict rules on any courtship but as, when she was not in hospital she was out working, these could not be easily enforced. She gave way when Linda started dating a fifteen-year-old named Jimmy Carter who worked with his father as a rag-and-bone man.

The problem was when he came round he smelt of horse manure and Lily insisted that he take a bath to quell the stench. It was Jimmy who introduced Alan to smoking cigarettes.

Alan was hit in the eye in an accident in the school gym. The injury did not seem serious, but he managed to persuade his mother to keep him off school for four months. This put an added strain on her finances as she had to provided his meals, rather than have him stuff himself for free at school. He filled his time playing his guitar, inventing his own football league and producing his own soccer magazine called *Soccer News*. By the time he returned to school he was well behind and never caught up academically.

When the money from Steve dried up completely, Linda and Jimmy went to confront Steve who, reluctantly, paid some of what he owed. Vera then announced that she was pregnant. When Lily heard about this, she insisted that Alan go and see his father too, if only to keep in contact with his half-sister when she came along. Alan resolutely refused, though Linda continued to see him to force money from him and see her half-sister Sandra. It was only much later that Alan realized Linda's real motive was to try and protect Sandra from what she had gone through.

Jimmy's older brother Johnny, a milkman, gave Alan a Saturday job, which was then extended to cover the Sunday-morning round. His job was to collect the empties and pick up the money settling each household's weekly bill. For lunch, Alan and Johnny shared a Swiss roll, washed down with a pint of milk. They collected from some of Rachman's more run-down establishments. One of them was 10 Ruston Place, which had previously been Rillington Place where at least seven women had been murdered by John Reginald Christie in the early 1950s.

Johnson earned 10 shillings a week. Lily refused to take any of it. As money was always tight, she had also taught the children to keep their eyes on the ground. One day, Alan found nearly ten shillings in coins on the pavement outside a betting shop. As he could no longer go and seen QPR on a Saturday, the money he did not save was spent on football publications.

Back at school, Johnson played football as goalkeeper for his house. In this capacity, he faced Malcolm Macdonald, losing his place in the team after letting in five goals. Despite this humiliation, he looked forward to football practice. This involved a trip to the school's playing fields in Roehampton and got him away from school for an afternoon. It was all the more welcome as the playing fields were shared with Carlyle Grammar School for Girls.

In the summer of 1962, Johnson went on holiday, visiting in Denmark courtesy of the Children's Country Holiday Fund. On the crossing, they were hit by a storm and everyone was seasick. They stayed in an agricultural college and were taken on improving trips to the Lurpak dairy and the Lego factory. Also on the trip was the bully who had stolen his box of bus tickets when he was six. He now demanded the Danish kroner Johnson had been given as pocket money.

Johnson would have been reluctant to break the unwritten rule and grass the bully up to a teacher. But the students running the trip were not teachers. They beat the bully until he confessed, then hung him upside down until the stolen money came cascading from his pockets. Other children were warned that they could expect the same treatment if they bullied or stole.

The rest of the holiday Johnson compared to an Enid Blyton adventure. The English boys played endless internationals against Danish boys. This gave them the opportunity to show off in front of the girls in their party. Soon Johnson was going on long country walks holding hands with Edna, who was from a council estate in Whitechapel. They kissed and promised to stay in touch when they got back to England, but after another choppy voyage home they never saw each other again. Back in London, Lily, who met the boat train at Liverpool Street, wanted to know why every other kid was carrying a Lego set. Alan had been given one at the factory too, but had traded his for twenty cigarettes.

While he had been way, Lily had put an ad in the lonely-hearts column of the *Kensington Post*. As a result, she met Ron, a builder who owned a bungalow in Romford. Linda and Alan took against him, but Lily appeared accommodating, perhaps thinking that he could save her from the squalid conditions they were still living in. She agreed that they would go to his house for Christmas. He would provide the food; she would cook. But the bird he had bought was a goose. Lily had never even seen a goose before. Preparing it was a nightmare. Then, when it was in the oven, it caught fire. The meal was a disaster and, in the heat of the moment, Ron called her a stupid woman. As there were no trains or buses on Christmas Day, they had to stay the night. After Ron had driven them to station the following day, Lily never saw him again.

This curtailed young Alan's amorous opportunities too. While at Ron's house, his flirtatious daughter had invited him to visit her in her bedroom. It was an invitation that he did not take up, but suspected that Linda's boyfriend Jimmy, who had also seen the note, might have gone in his place. Soon after Linda explained the facts of life to him. The details appalled him, so perhaps it was best that he had not gone.

At school, Alan's favourite subject was English, where the class read George Orwell's *Animal Farm*. His English teacher also taught Religious Education, spending the lessons railing again racial segregation in South Africa. Having seen racism first-hand in Notting Hill, Alan was an easy convert to the anti-apartheid cause, though not to Christianity. Under the guidance of his English teacher, Alan also took to the stage in the school play.

Another new teacher also helped foster Alan's burgeoning political awareness. He was a Hungarian who had fled his homeland when Soviet tanks had crushed the uprising in 1956. He was a socialist, he said, not a communist, and explained the difference.

Alan had another long period off school after a near-fatal appendicitis, which was only caught in the nick of time. He spent a fortnight in hospital listening to the radio. This was where he first heard the Beatles' "Please Please Me". They were a favourite because they came from his mother's hometown. Here, at last, was home-grown talent, not a pale imitation of an American act. Alan was hooked.

Chapter Four – The Loss of Lily

Alan returned from hospital during the severe winter of 1962-63 in their freezing flat. It was the coldest winter since 1740. Every day, he had to trundle an old pram rescued from the tip round to the local coal merchants where the coal was still hauled by magnificent carthorses. The flat now possessed a two-bar electric heater, but it used too much electricity to be kept on for long.

As always, Lily insisted that Alan ask for the coal on tick, something that acutely embarrassed him. When this was refused, he had just enough cash to buy enough coal to keep the fire in the back room lit for a day, with a few extra lumps to be saved for Sunday when the coal merchants was closed. On the trip, he kept his eyes peels for other lumps to scavenge.

January 1963 was the coldest month since 1814 and the country was brought to a standstill by snow, ice and free fog. No football could be played, so the pools companies had to set up a panel to generate the results to keep them in business.

By March, when the thaw set it, Alan was passed fit for school. That May, a week before his thirteenth birthday, he overcame his enduring antipathy for Chelsea and went to Stamford Bridge to see the great Stanley Matthews, who was then playing for Stoke City in the twilight of his career.

Linda and her friends had become Mods, while Alan, like others of his generation, had discovered the records of black American R&B, such as B.B. King, Bo Diddley, John Lee Hooker, Howlin' Wolf and Muddy Waters, who had been all but forgotten in their own country. This music formed the backbone of the "British invasion" of the United States in 1964.

Alan, though, was a particular fan of Chuck Berry and bought American imports in a record store in Roehampton. These were borrowed by Linda's sharp-suited friends, earning her little brother inordinate respect. As soon as he could afford it, Alan was determined to become a Mod.

At school, Alan was surrounded by middle-class boys desperate to rebel. He had nothing to rebel against. In fact, thanks to the Beatles and kitchen-sink dramas on the stage and television, it was becoming fashionable to be working class. This gave him enough clout to form a band, the Vampires, who rehearsed in the basement of classmate Colin James's home in Parsons Green. It was also a place they could innocently entertain girls.

In the early 1960s, being in a band was the thing to do. Everyone wanted to jump on the bandwagon. One of the other boys at Sloane Grammar was Steve Hackett, who went on to become lead guitarist with Genesis and the supergroup GTR.

The Vampires sought further inspiration in the 100 Club in Oxford Street, Soho's Marquee Club and the Crawdaddy Club in Richmond. They saw the Rolling Stones, Georgie Fame and the Blue Flames, the Pretty Things, the Yardbirds and, later, Rod Stewart.

They began growing their hair long and customizing their school blazers with six-inch vents – the latest Mod fashion – inviting a caning from a disapproving headmaster. They also began hanging around out the World's End pub in King's Road, where the Rolling Stones were said to drink, but they never saw them there.

Alan and Colin had planned to take a holiday hitchhiking along the south coast. That was what rebellious youth did in those days. But instead they were persuaded to join the rest of Colin's family in a house-swap in Sussex. There Alan read *Goldfinger* in a single sitting. He was just hitting puberty when the country was engulfed in the Profumo sex scandal, some of which took place nearby in Notting Hill.

Lily's health was deteriorating and her GP petitioned the Housing Department to find her a council house as a medical priority. Linda quit school to get a job and bring in more money, while finding time to train as a nurse. Then Lily was told of a new procedure that might alleviate her heart condition. Without this ground-breaking operation, she would not live much longer, she was told. However, as it meant she would be hospitalized for at least three months, she refused.

Despite her determination to keep on working and Linda's contribution, Lily fell ever deeper into debt. She took to playing bingo in the forlorn hope of improving her lot with a big win.

With Johnny Carter, Alan began delivering paraffin two nights a week to bring in extra money. As a result, he stank of the stuff. But as part of the deal, he got a pie and chips on the way home. The money he earned was spent on records and paperback detective novels.

Linda's new boyfriends, the manager of a local electrical shop, introduced Alan to the records of Bob Dylan who immediately became his latest hero. Soon he could recite the words of Dylan's songs off by heart. He also had the album *Green Onions* by Booker T. and the MGs.

Both the gas and the electricity had been cut off when Linda went out on a date. Alan, who had been left at home in the freezing flat to keep an eye on his mother, grew concerned about her. When Linda came home, Lily was delirious and cried out to Steve, cursing him. The doctor was called. He summoned an ambulance.

With Lily in hospital again, sixteen-year-old Linda did her best to try and handle the family's calamitous financial situation. She made arrangements for the gas and electricity to be turned on again and was rehired part-time by the shop where she had earlier paid Lily's slate. The shopkeeper, hearing of their dire circumstances, gave them a box of groceries.

Now Lily had no choice. Without radical heart surgery, she would die. What's more, she would have to stay in the hospital until the operation was done. It was months away. Linda and Alan were careful who they told of their situation, fearing that they would be taken in to care or – worse – have to go and live with Steve. Besides the Vampires were too busy trying to cover the latest Beatle's single. Then came the news that President Kennedy had been assassinated.

Over Christmas, local families and shops rallied round. Lily wanted to come home to be with her children for the holiday, but the doctors would not let her return to the unhealthy conditions there. So Linda and Alan spent Christmas Day alone again. This time, they remembered to unwrap the chicken before they cooked it.

They visited the hospital on Christmas afternoon. Lily was cheerful, promising them that they would have their own home the following year. On the way home, Linda told Alan that Lily still had not signed the consent form for the operation and asked him what he thought. Alan said that, if the operation was Lily's only chance, she should go ahead. When they got home, the woman upstairs gave them sandwiches in front of a blazing fire. It was the first time Alan had tasted turkey.

Left to his own devices, Alan's circle of friends grew. They all seemed to come from families that were loving and stable – and a good deal better off. He gained a reputation of being bookish, so much so that the German mother of a friend gave him a copy of Dante's *Inferno*, which he found unfathomable, though he did not let on.

The night before her operation, Lily wept openly in front of other people. It was the only time Alan remembered her doing so. She still had not signed the consent forms. She was afraid. At forty-two, she was now at the age both her mother and grandmother had died. Linda did her best to persuade her to sign the papers.

The following day, after the operation, Lily was in intensive case in a medically induced coma. A week later, after a second operation, her kidneys failed. Linda, who herself was devastated by the news, then had to tell Alan. He was unable to take in what he was being told and found himself unable to shed a tear. It was only years later that he found he could cry at the thought of his precious, long-dead mother.

As always, Linda took charge. She informed Lily's family in Liverpool, took time off from work and told Alan's school that he would not be back there for a while. There was the death certificate to handle, the birth certificate to find and the funeral arrangements to organize. The cost was fortunately covered by an insurance policy. In the mortuary, they discovered that Lily's wedding ring had to be cut off her finger and they were handed her dentures. With the advent of the NHS, it was common among working-class people to have all their teeth taken out and replaced with false ones. Linda and Alan also had to make the rounds to inform Steve's family, but declined any offers of help.

Lily was to be cremated. Aunt Jean and Uncle George would be coming down from Liverpool for the funeral and offered to take the children back with, but Linda and Alan did not want to go.

They stayed at the Coxes until the funeral where, at long last, the book case was unlocked and Alan was lent a leather-bound copy of *David Copperfield*. When their aunts and uncles arrived, they were in shock. They had known nothing of Lily's heart condition and were doubly shocked by the living conditions she had been reduced to in Walmer Road.

Friends and family were not given to displays of emotion. However, on the Saturday before Lily's funeral, after they had finished the milk round, Johnny Carter, who had somehow acquired a large collection of musical instruments, asked Alan to pick one. Alan chose a Vox. It was his first electric guitar and Linda's new boyfriend provided an amplifier.

Wearing a black knitted tie that Steve had left behind, Alan attended the funeral at All Souls, Kensal Green with his sister and a large contingent of scousers. In the cemetery they spotted Steve. At his request, Linda left Alan with him for a few moments. Steve made his apologies and gave Alan a key ring with a little football attached to it. It was the last they ever saw of each other.

Afterwards, Linda and Alan went to stay in Liverpool for a week, but then returned to London, determined to go on living together on their own in Walmer Road. However, they soon received a notice addressed to her mother that the building was going to be demolished as it was no longer fit for human habitation. She was to be rehoused in a three-bedroom semi in Welwyn Garden City.

This meant they could no longer stay on in Walmer Road and they were too young to take over the house in Welwyn. Though Linda had been one of the mainstays of the family for years, she was still considered to be a child. They were told that she would be sent to Dr Barnado's, while Alan would be put in foster care. Linda refused to budge, insisting that they stayed together. After all, they had been taking care of themselves for years.

The council reluctantly gave way and agreed to rehouse them, provided that they were visited regularly by a social worker and an adult stood guarantor. Uncle Jim agreed to do that and they were offered a flat at the top of a tower block in Hammersmith. When they visited it, they found it in a worse state than Walmer Road and they refused it. Eventually they were offered a two-bedroom maisonette at the south end of Wandsworth Bridge. It had a bathroom and an indoor toilet. For Linda and Alan this was opulence.

Steve had offered to help with the rent, but his contribution soon dried up. Nevertheless, Linda somehow managed. The neighbours were hostile though, resentful that a flat had been given to two teenagers when, in their eyes, other families were more deserving. As a result, the flat was vandalized and regularly burgled. But they could not risk complaining to the police or their social worker in case the authorities reverted to their plan to put them in care.

Slowly Alan began to enjoy school. The new English teacher engaged the pupils with contemporary literature and took them to the theatre and musicals. He encouraged Alan's interest in reading and introduced him to new writers he thought he would enjoy. Nevertheless, Alan wanted to leave school as soon as possible. Linda was against this and turned up at parents' evenings to tell the teachers so. But Alan was determined to get on with his career as rock star.

Chapter Five – The Road from Rock

When he left school at the age of fifteen in July 1965, another grammar-school boy named Harold Wilson was prime minister and Alan began taking an interest in politics – particularly the radical reforms the Labour government were pushing through. When he got his first proper job as a postal clerk at the headquarters of Remington Razors in High Street Kensington, he bought *The Times* to read on the way to work.

After six months, he got another job in the Tesco's warehouse in Hammersmith with Andrew Wiltshire, a friend from school who owned a drum kit. With Danny Curtis, a childhood acquaintance from Notting Hill, they formed a band called The Area. Danny had a van to transport the gear and put an ad in *Melody Maker*. This bought them a lead guitarist named Tony Kearns from Chester and bassist Ian Clark, a Scottish music student at London University.

The line-up had just got together when Alan's Vox was stolen in one of their frequent break-ins. But Lily had left £40 for Alan, which Linda had intended to give him when he was older. He used the money to buy a red Höfner Verythin from a shop in Soho.

Soon they were playing Wednesday nights at the Pavilion pub opposite Wormwood Scrubs, even though they were too young to drink there. They also supported Fifth Dynasty and the Symbols, who had a couple of minor hits in the 1960s, which took them to gigs in other pubs, clubs and colleges.

While Alan's musical career seemed to be taking off, Linda got married. Her new husband found them a house in Watford. This lost them the maisonette in Wandsworth and Alan returned to Notting Hill. He moved in with the Coxes and shared a room with his old friend Tony, who now had a Lambretta and a parka with "The Who" emblazoned on the back.

While they were committed to the band, Alan hedged his bets and answered wanted ads in *Melody Maker*. He auditioned for Peter Jay and Jaywalkers, a band who did live covers of hit records when "needle time" was still restricted on the BBC. At the audition, he played The Beatles' "This Boy" and felt he had got the gig. But weeks passed and he had not heard from them. Eventually, he gave up.

At Tesco's, Alan was asked over temporarily as warehouse manager without any raise in pay. After three months, when this was not forthcoming, he walked out. It was ten days before Christmas and the seasonal rush was on. His supervisor offered to take him back, but Alan felt he had been exploited and stood his ground. Within two weeks, he found himself another job stacking shelves in a self-service convenience store in East Sheen where, the following Christmas, the boss bought him *Sergeant Pepper's Lonely Hearts Club Band* as a present. Ever a fan of the four working-class lads from Liverpool, he had saved up to buy a collarless Beatles jacket, but stopped wearing it when the Fab Four stopped wearing theirs.

By then the wholesale demolition of the slums around Notting Hill was underway and the new council blocks were rising. The Coxes too were being rehoused, out in Roehampton. There would not be room for Alan to live there with them. Instead, he rented a room in a large flat in Hammersmith, which he shared with a widow and her son – though he never saw them and kept himself to himself. He had the occasional girlfriend, but the would-be rock god now lived exclusively for the band.

Danny hired a sound studio in Denmark Street and they recorded one of Alan's songs, "I Have Seen", and "Hard Life" written by Tony and Ian. The demo was hawked around the record companies to no avail. Pop entrepreneur Don Arden, who managed the Small Faces, showed some interest in releasing it as a single and hiring The Area as a support act. But the band's equipment was stolen from the Four Feathers where the Small Faces used to practise. Luckily, Alan had taken his Höfner Verythin home with him, but he lost his amplifier. Neither Alan or the other band members could afford to replace their gear, so that was the end of The Area.

Some months later, Alan was recruited by The In-Betweens, a semi-professional band of mixed Caribbean and Asian origins, fronted by a beautiful Indo-German girl named Carmen. They played a mixture of pop and soul, and had a regular Friday-night gig in the Pied Horse in the Angel, Islington, across the road from the Post Office's Northern District sorting office where the bassist Sham Hassan worked.

In 1968, The In-Betweens were on the rise. They were gigging regularly and A&R men from the major record labels were coming to see them. They were auditioned in a studio in Shepherd's Bush. A recording contract was in prospect, along with a TV documentary about the mixed-race band. It all came to nothing when, once again, the band's equipment was stolen. This time Alan's Höfner disappeared with everything else. Again this sounded the death knell of the band.

Sham wanted Alan to form another band with him. But at a New Year's party at Linda's, Alan had met Judy Cox. Although she was also from Notting Hill, she was not related to Tony Cox's family. Four years older than Alan, she was also the offspring off a drunken, abusive father. Her mother had died when she was just sixteen-months old. While her brothers disappeared into children's homes, she had been brought up by her grandparents. Alan had met her before, briefly, when she had been studying nursing with Linda. At the time, she had been seeing an Italian trainee teacher. When she fell pregnant, he high-tailed it back to Italy, leaving her to bring up her baby daughter Natalie alone, except for the help of her aging grandmother.

Alan and Judy started dating. Despite Linda's objections – she still harboured Lily's ambition for Alan to study to be a draftsman – they decided to marry in July, a few weeks after he turned eighteen. Later he adopted Natalie, so now he had wife and child to support. After their turbulent childhoods, both of them craved stability and domesticity.

The store where he worked in East Sheen was taken over by Tesco's. Alan did not want to work for them again. He was on the lookout for another steady job when Sham suggested that he come and work with him in the Post Office. The idea appealed.

Shortly after his eighteenth birthday, Alan went for an interview at the GPO recruiting office in Lavender Hill. The General Post Office was still a government department then. It was not until the following year that the Post Office became a public corporation. In both cases, the pay was poor and there were plenty of vacancies. Alan got the job and was sent off on a two-week training course in King's Cross.

After he was married, Alan moved back into Notting Hill once more, moving into the house in Camelford Road that Judy shared with her grandmother. Thinking that her granddaughter could have done better for herself, she treated him with ill-concealed disdain.

He managed to get a posting to Barnes, a leafy suburb he had first seen on his daily bus journey from Hammersmith to East Sheen. Every morning he would cycle the five miles there, ready to start work at the crack of dawn.

On Christmas Eve 1968, Judy gave birth to their daughter Emma. Now with a growing family, Alan needed all the overtime he could get and had left behind him any idea of being a rock star. He would continue writing songs and thought he may even return to performing at some point, but he had reconciled himself to being a postman until he retired.

Chapter Six – Mr. Postman

While the Royal Mail had a huge delivery office on Barnes Green, only thirty people worked there. It was a haven of peace while the rest of the world seemed to be erupting with demonstrations against the Vietnam war and marches for civil rights. Student rebellions and the talk of revolution meant little to Alan and Judy. They were concerned with settling into respectable family life.

Barnes itself was a civilized backwater, home to established actors, artists, writers, broadcasters and the occasional government minister. As the latest recruit, Johnson's job was to cover the deliveries of men who were ill or on leave.

Young and quick on his feet, Johnson could be back in the office by 9 am, ready for a leisurely breakfast and a game of snooker in the canteen. Older hands warned him not to be so quick, otherwise more streets would be added to the round. To delay his return, he would pop across the bridge to have a cup of tea in Hammersmith which was beyond the purview of the officious inspector who checked up on the delivery men.

Most of his fellow postmen were ex-servicemen, though they never talked of their wartime experiences. One former Guardsman had previously worked as a postman in SW1. One of his duties there was to collect the parchment scrolls detailing that day's business from

Parliament and deliver it to Buckingham Palace. Johnson was impressed.

All the postmen were characters. One man claimed to have been regularly seduced on his round, which seemed unlikely. Another told of a lady who stood in her bedroom window bare-breasted each morning combing her hair. When Johnson stood in on his round one day, he discovered that this story was true.

On Johnson's first day at Barnes, he was approached by the Union of Post Office Workers and signed up, both for membership and for a UPW policy that would supplement his pension when he retired. His experience at Tesco's convinced him that he needed the protection of the union.

While the supervisor shirked his duties, Johnson was impressed with the union representative who never cut corners either in the union duties or the work he did for the post office, while earning considerably less money than his management counterpart.

While Johnson took every bit of overtime he could get – including the extra two hours he got every morning to clean the toilets – he still took time to read, now concentrating on modern history.

He also became incensed by injustices in the Post Office pay grades. The basic pay for young recruits was a pittance which, for postmen, rose to a maximum at twenty-four. But if a recruit joined at twenty-five, they would go straight on the maximum, earning considerably more than the juniors who had several years experience.

This disdain for the young extended to his work colleagues. In their heated political debates, the older postmen would brook no interjection from "juveniles" like Johnson. But while others read the *Daily Express* and the *Daily Mirror*, Johnson still read *The Times*, though he did so in secret, not to draw the fire of his comrades. He also read copies of *Newsweek* and *Punch*, slipping them temporarily from their lose paper sleeves before he delivered them.

However, he did not pay much attention to the *Post*, the union's monthly magazine, so he was surprised when the men were summoned to a union meeting and told they had been called out on a one-day strike in support of the overseas telegraph officers. They were in dispute with the management who were attempting to foist a productivity agreement on them. It was to be the union's first national strike.

The only time Alan got to voice his political opinions was with his brother-in-law, Linda's husband Mike, who he described as a "working-class Tory". While Mike condemned Enoch Powell's avowed racist "rivers of blood" speech, he supported Edward Heath's attempt to take Britain into what was then the Common Market. But when Alan spoke up in favour of the Post Office strike, Mike said it sounded as if he was on his way to become "a Bolshie shop steward".

Johnson spent the day of the strike typing up a poem for publication. He sent it to *Spring Poets '69*, a vanity publication. Inclusion cost £5 – half a week's wages. Johnson does not claim that it was a great poem, only that it was a good deal better than most of the others that had been included.

The following day, he and other men made up the day's pay they had lost, clearing the backlog on overtime. Meanwhile, the Postmaster General John Stonehouse – who later faked his own death so he could live with his mistress in Australia – offered to negotiate. *The Times* described this as "capitulation".

The union representative congratulated the staff at Barnes, but the one man who had broken the strike was sent to Coventry. No one talked to him. He was ignored. Johnson later said he felt ashamed for having colluded in his exclusion.

Five months after the strike, Johnson applied to become a Post Office driver and was sent to the driving school in Croydon. As Post Office vans did not have synchromesh gearboxes, drivers had to learn the complex technique of double declutching.

In the middle of his driving course, Johnson overslept. Fearing he would be late, he cycled furiously through the pouring rain without donning his Post Office oilskins. He arrived in the nick of time, but then passed out. His driving course was cancelled and he was sent for the medical he should have had when he first started work.

News came that Camelford Road was to be demolished. Alan and Judy were offered a council house in Slough, thirty miles west of London, while his belligerent mother-in-law was moved into sheltered accommodation.

Arriving in Slough, they were told by the local police that the Britwell Estate, where they had been offered a house, has a certain reputation for criminality. Could it be worse than the slums of Notting Hill? As they entered the estate, they saw a daub that read "Keep Britwell White." But the two-bedroom house itself, though boarded up and overgrown, was spacious and faced onto a little green. It was the sort of place Lily would have given her right arm for.

At the time, Johnson had not read John Betjeman's poem: "Come, friendly bombs, and fall on Slough!/ It isn't fit for humans now", but he had been brought up in a series of buildings that had been condemned. He knew what was fit for human habitation and what was not.

When his twelve-months probationary period with the Post Office was up, Alan got a transfer to the Slough sorting office. They moved home on 5 July 1969, the day the Rolling Stones gave a free concert in Hyde Park.

Moving in, they had no washing machine, no fridge, no vacuum cleaner and no phone. These things would have to be saved up for over many years. Memories of the tallyman coming round meant that the Johnsons eschewed buying on tick. However, there was a small coal-burning stove in the front room that, thanks to the thin walls, took the edge off the chill in the whole house. After the privations of Notting Hill, this was heaven.

Slough was a huge Post Office hub with a telephone exchange and a parcel office. The sorting office was undergoing the beginnings of automation. There was a rotating machine that separated the letters from the parcels and the sorters bundled up letters using elastic bands. In London, the men had refused to do this, tying each bundle with waxed string to avoid "de-skilling".

There were other techniques and terminology to learn and Johnson was given a week's training by Mr. Khan, an immigrant from East Pakistan, now Bangladesh. One of the first things he was told was not to leave his bicycle for a moment when delivering to his round on the Britwell Estate. Bicycles were always being stolen there. Though he found the Britwall Estate pleasant enough to live on, his round there was nowhere near as pleasant as it had been in Barnes.

The houses around the green were occupied by other young couples with children and they were soon in and out of each other's houses. Alan continued taking as much overtime as he could to support his family. This meant he saw little of them. He left for work at 5 a.m. and, after an afternoon shift in the parcels office, returned at 7.30 p.m., after the children were in bed. He regularly worked on Sundays for double time as well. Sometimes he would even cover the night shift on Fridays, working from 8 p.m. through to the end of his delivery round on Saturday.

Things improved when he managed to secure a round in the village of Burnham, which he could do on foot. It was like being back in Barnes again. Another Burnham postman would give him a lift to work in his three-wheeled Reliant Regal. Sometimes he would wake Alan, if he and Judy had been out for a few pints with the neighbours, by flinging pebbles as his bedroom window. Johnson was never a natural early riser.

Mopeds were being introduced for delivery men. Johnson got one. He then rode out to Burnham under his own steam, before beginning his rounds. It also gave him the luxury of returning home for lunch with the kids, though he never sought permission to take the moped home, figuring it must be against the rules.

The afternoon shifts in the parcels office was dirty and gruelling, but the men worked at high speed, earning themselves time to pay darts or cards for a bit before they clocked off.

When Johnson was not working or watching TV with his children, he was reading, now substituting political theory for modern history. The world then was divided ideologically between communism and capitalism; he had lived through the Cuban Missile Crisis of 1962 when the world teetered on the brink of nuclear annihilation and sought to understand why. After the serious reading was done, he still devoured the odd novel.

In the spirit of the time, he had a brief flirtation with hippydom and Judy bought him an Incredible String Band album for Christmas in 1969, along with his first razor. Although already a father, he remained a fresh-faced youth until the age of nineteen. He also found himself eligible to vote as the Representation of the People Act of 1969 reduced the age of majority in the UK from twenty-one to eighteen. He voted for the first time in 1970. While Labour held Slough, the Conservatives under Edward Heath won in the country.

A revolution was then blowing through the Post Office. The Post Office Act of 1969 abolished the position of Postmaster General and transferred his power to the new Minister of Post and

Telecommunications. He would appoint a chairman and board to run the new corporation, though it had yet to undergo the "white heat" of technological change promised by Harold Wilson in 1963.

Other things remained staunchly old-fashioned. Although there were an increasing number of Asians working for the Post Office, they sat apart from the white workers in the canteen, and there were no women workers, apart from among the casual staff taken on at Christmas.

Trouble was brewing among the ranks. After the Tory victory in 1970, the new government sacked the Post Office chairman Viscount Hall, who was thought to have been too sympathetic to the work force. As a result, there were strikes. Heath believed that he had a mandate to tame the unions. Sparks began to fly when the UPW put in a claim for a wage rise of fifteen per cent and the Post Office countered with an offer of seven. That Christmas, the union advised workers to rack up all the overtime pay they could as they would be in for a long strike in the New Year.

This was a worrying prospect for the Johnson family. There was another mouth to feed. Judy gave birth to a son, Jamie, on 10 January 1971. Alan wrote a song in celebration. There was no statutory paternity leave in those days. Johnson got his by happenstance. The UPW came out on strike on the twentieth.

Johnson was a strong supporter of the strike. The Post Office were claiming that average wages were high, but they were including overtime payments. Johnson was also suffering wage discrimination as, despite his two years' experience, he was still only twenty. The union sought to do away with the old age-related incremental scales too.

At the beginning of the strike, along with three hundred others, Johnson queued outside the benefits office in Slough. Strikers were allowed to claim for dependents, but not for themselves. Initially, Johnson was turned away – he did not appear old enough to have dependents. But when he produced his marriage certificate and the birth certificates of the children he was given £12 17s 6d a week. This was 7s 6d more than his basic wage, though not nearly as much as he got when all his overtime was added in.

None of the postmen broke the strike, but some of the telephonists, who were also members of the UPW, did. But, in Slough, the strike was a good-natured affair. Johnson and the other pickets did not shout slogans at them. They exchanged polite greetings instead.

Each week the strikers would be bussed up to Hyde Park for a rally. Johnson was not impressed by the middle-class students who tried to recruit the strikers to join the International Socialists or other far-left organizations. Johnson wanted an extra £3 a week, not a revolution. There were also local meetings in the community centre, but the debate there was largely confined to who got what from the hardship fund.

The leader of the strike was the UPW's general secretary Tom Jackson, still remembered for his huge handlebar moustache. Johnson was an instant fan. The strikers believed that they had a powerful weapon in the forthcoming Decimal Day on 15 February 1971, when the old currency of pounds, shillings and pence, with

240 pence to the pound, was to be replaced with a new one of pounds and pence, with just one hundred pence to the pound. The Post Office with its Girobank was thought to be a vital part of the changeover and, they thought, it was vital for the postal service to deliver leaflets explaining the details of the new currency.

The government had a weapon of its own. It temporarily suspended the Post Office's monopoly on postal delivery, but the private companies that stepped in proved expensive and unreliable.

Johnson was not the most militant of strikers. Though he did his share on the picket line, he spent most of his time with his children, or reading Dylan Thomas.

After seven weeks, the strike was called off. The dispute was to be settled by a committee of enquiry. There had been no vote to go out on strike. That had been an executive decision. But there was a vote to return. Johnson voted against. Nevertheless, he retained his admiration for Tom Jackson who had showed flair early in the strike when presenting the union's case to the public and the courage to lead the men back to work when he realized that the strike would inevitably end in failure. It had been the biggest industrial action, in terms of man-hours lost, since the General Strike of 1926. And to clear the backlog, there was the added bonus of unlimited overtime.

In the end, the committee of inquiry recommended a pay increase of nine per cent. However, it also adjusted the incremental scales, so Johnson himself would receive a higher hike in pay.

Chapter Seven – Part of the Union

After the strike, Johnson returned to working seven days a week, often putting in two shifts on a Sunday. His only relaxation was a drink with his neighbours on a Friday night, watching QPR's home games with a car-load of other fans from the sorting office and a kick-about on a Sunday morning as captain of South Postal FC, followed by a beer and a game of bingo, then cards, at the British Legion. After that, he took a bottle of light ale home to Judy who was cooking the Sunday lunch. Then it was off to work, or a snooze in front of the telly after watching *The Big Match*. Otherwise socializing was confined to regular house parties with neighbours, or a Saturday-night trip to a local pub, if they could get a babysitter.

After reading Dylan Thomas, Johnson became quite a fan of poetry. "Elegy Written in a Country Church Yard" had been written by Thomas Gray in St. Giles parish churchyard in Stoke Poges nearby. Johnson took Judy and the kids there for the two-hundredth anniversary of Gray's death.

Johnson returned to his drivers' training course. After five attempts, he passed his driving test and bought a Ford Anglia, which he parked proudly on the green in front of the house. This gave them the opportunity to visit family and friends.

Though he was perfectly content with being a postman for the rest of his life – he enjoyed the camaraderie – Johnson continued to strum on his Spanish guitar and write songs. Later, he bought a twelve-string Eko acoustic – not another electric guitar. This was a tacit admission that his career in rock and roll was over.

Meanwhile the pitiless routine of work still dominated his life. He got three weeks holiday a year, along with the ten days sick leave without a medical certificate that all the postmen took.

After five years in the job, Johnson was feeling a little restless. He applied for promotion to Postman Higher Grade – with a pay rise – and was sent to the Post Office training school at Bletchley Park, the home of Britain's wartime code-breakers. At the time, the code of secrecy surrounding those who had worked there had just been lifted. There he was taught the more specialist procedures he would need to know as a PHG.

But his promotion had not quelled his discontent. Back in Slough he joined the Labour Party along with his neighbour, ambulanceman Mick Pearson. Harold Wilson was then back in Downing Street, but as the head of a minority government, he was hardly in the position to continue the radical reforms he had made in his first administration.

Johnson got hold of a copy of *Das Kapital* and began studying Marxism. He had little time for the politicians in the Labour party. At the time, his political hero was Jimmy Reid, the communist trade unionist who had led a work-in at Upper Clyde Shipbuilders to victory in 1972. Reid had left school at fourteen to become a shipyard apprentice and had risen to become a national figure. But while they shared a love of music, football, books and poetry,

Johnson knew that the Communist Party of Great Britain was not for him. He did not see how a communist state could be a free society.

He also had discussions with the local recruiter for the Workers' Revolutionary Party, then much in vogue under the leadership of Vanessa and Corin Redgrave. It was one of the half-dozen leftist splinter groups who battled it out over ideology. While they all purported to stick up for the working class, their adherents seemed to be uniformly middle class who had no support among those they claimed to champion.

Then in 1975, Jimmy Reid quit the CPGB and joined the Labour Party, and Johnson's flirtation with the left was at an end. He now took a more active role in the union. The following February, Johnson was elected chairman of the Slough Amalgamated Branch of the Union of Post Office Workers. He managed to conclude his first AGM just as the pubs opened.

Then he set about revising the rules, insisting that the branch committees met more often and ensuring that the members were kept informed. Everything had to be done in accordance with the *ABC of Chairmanship*, written by the distinguished general secretary of the TUC, Walter Citrine. He also visited the sick and generally looked after his members.

In May 1976, he attended the annual conference of the UPW at the Winter Gardens, Bournemouth. It was the first time he had ever stayed in a hotel.

The UPW was still led by Tom Jackson who, after the comprehensive defeat of 1971, had gone on to negotiate a number of excellent pay deals. The opening session was addressed by the new Prime Minister Jim Callaghan. Six days of debate followed. Johnson enjoyed the theatre of the occasion, along with the horse-trading and the socializing.

The union opened up a new world that was far more satisfying than anything promotion in the Post Office could offer. He resigned as a PHG and went back to working long hours of overtime to make up the difference, consoling himself by taking a country round. A local newsagent paid him extra to deliver newspapers to his customers. He also delivered bags of coal, groceries and the sacks of manure to be used on the garden. One family left the cat food out, with a tin-opener, so he could feed their cat when they were away.

He attended another UPW conference at the end of 1976, but again did not pluck up the courage to speak. However, the union did present him with another opportunity – that was to continue his education. As a union official he was eligible to take any number of correspondence courses provided free of charge by the TUC. However, what correspondence courses could not teach him was the oratory that he had seen on display at union conferences.

He took the plunge at a branch meeting called over a proposed boycott of mail and telephone calls to and from South Africa after schoolchildren protesting being taught in Afrikaans had been shot down in Soweto in 1976. The anti-apartheid movement was something Johnson cared passionately about, but most of his members were against the boycott.

He addressed them in the canteen at the sorting office. It was hardly a prestigious venue and not designed for oratory. When the speech he had written was failing, he abandoned it and spoke from the heart. At the end, he received a round of applause. Nevertheless, the members voted narrowly against him.

While his love of rock music never deserted him, Johnson broadened his taste to include classical and he started a collection with Mussorgsky's *Pictures at an Exhibition*. He was soon surprised by the number of workmates who shared his new-found love of classical music and poetry.

Meanwhile, he was tireless in his union work. During his working day, Johnson would speak to his fellow postal workers and write down any complaint or comment they had in a notebook. He made a point of getting back to everyone whose criticism or remark he had logged.

Johnson's debating skills were honed in the kitchen of Hicknham Farm where Mrs Rayham extended her hospitality to visiting tradesman. When she learnt that he was a union official, she voiced her anti-union, anti-state supported industries and anti-Common Market views. At first, Johnson was too polite to reply. Later, when a binman joined the conversation, pointing out that large European money subsidies were given to farmers, she rounded on him with detailed arguments on the importance of agriculture. Johnson soon found he could join in and such robust debates became a feature of his mornings.

His round also took in Dorneywood, the country retreat of the Home Secretary. Suspicious packages had already been winnowed out at the sorting office and, when he arrived there, he was simply waved through by the security guard. While he was never allowed inside, he would take a break there, perhaps reading a novel, before returning to do his evening collections. He enjoyed these quiet moments in the countryside as much as he did the hurly-burly of union work.

At the 1977 annual conference, there was a motion to abolish the remaining incremental scales. Although this did not affect Johnson directly, as he was now twenty-seven and on full pay, the matter still wrangled. This time he got to his feet, waved his agenda paper in the air and was called to the rostrum.

He knew that reading from a prepared script did him no favours so, instead, he had scribbled some notes on a pad he could refer to if he dried up. He presented his case, using examples from his personal experience. However, the national officer who answered his speech pointed out that pay was now subject to the all-encompassing "social contract" the unions had negotiated with the government. Consequently, minor adjustments could not be made and the conference rejected the proposal. Nevertheless, Johnson had put his toe in the water.

The following year, he decided to put his name forward for the executive council. No lesser intermediate role would do. He wanted to be in the centre of things. But he had to get the nomination of his branch and was too self-effacing to ask. Instead he accepted the position of assistant district organizer.

At the time the Callaghan government was in disarray. While it tried to fend off the demands of the unions, it was under attack by the Bennite left. Equal opportunities legislation had come into effect, allowing postwomen to join the staff at Slough. But at the Grunwick mail-order film possessing plant in Cricklewood, the workforce of mainly Asian women were trying to force union recognition. The UPW intervened, blacking the company's mail and forcing the owner to go to arbitration.

The legality of the UPW's South African boycott was still being contested. But when arbitration in the Grunwick case failed, the UPW were reluctant to re-impose the embargo for fear of further legal sanctions. However, the London District Council under John Taylor and Derek Walsh – two of Johnson's allies at conference – defied the executive and backed action by the postmen of Cricklewood, resulting in a lock-out and a mass picket of the Grunwick plant by Yorkshire miners who had been bussed in. Taylor and Walsh were then fined by the union. At that year's conference in the Winter Garden, Blackpool, Johnson spoke up for his friends.

Asked to move an amendment, Johnson approached the rostrum, only to find he was speaking to the wrong motion and had to retreat in disarray. Moments later, Tom Jackson, who had left the platform, came over to offer consolation. He also asked, in a loud voice, whether Johnson had thought of standing for the executive council. The rest of the Slough delegation were within earshot. Over lunch, they offered to nominate the following year. On his third attempt, he was elected.

In the intervening years, with Tom Jackson's encouragement, he honed his oratory. However, he found that he was not a natural showman and only found the requisite eloquence when he was talking about something he cared about. He also claimed that he did not make deals for votes in the conference bars like other candidates.

But Johnson had another political role closer to home. When Natalie failed her eleven-plus, he did not want his daughters to go to the local secondary school, Warrenfield Comprehensive, which had a bad reputation. Instead, he got her into Haymill, where he became a school governor. Then came the news that the school had been earmarked for closure and he joined the fight to save it – though this eventually failed.

He gave up smoking and used the money he saved to extend his record collection – even venturing into punk with albums by Elvis Costello and Joe Jackson. Meanwhile, the political landscape was changing. Callaghan's government was plagued by the "winter of discontent" and in March 1979 it lost a vote of confidence in the House of Commons. The ensuing election that May brought Margaret Thatcher to power.

Active in the local Labour Party, Johnson got to know the local MP, Joan Lestor, and drove her around during the campaign. The front room of the Johnsons' house was used as a Labour committee room on polling day. While until then he had only interested himself in political theory, now he saw the mechanics of getting the vote out.

Once Johnson had been elected to the executive committee of what was now called the Union of Communication Works in May 1981, he quit the sorting office. His early morning rounds were now over. He was now on permanent special leave from the Post Office to go about his union business.

Before his first meeting of the executive committee, Johnson found himself in the room alone with Tom Jackson. He had already sent a note of congratulation. Now he said he had high hopes for Johnson's future in the union.

The union's headquarters were in Clapham, an hour's drive from Slough. He would have an office there. Otherwise he was to teach at the union training schools, help resolve disputes, support national officers in their negotiations and attend conferences of sister unions around the world as a fraternal delegate.

Following the fall of the Callaghan government, Labour was under attack by a group of Trotskyite insurgents known as Militant tendency, formerly the Revolutionary Socialist League. They trashed anyone connected with the previous administration, with the exception of Tony Benn. Johnson found Benn articulate and persuasive, and agreed with a lot he had to say. But his refusal to stick up for former colleagues smacked of treachery, Johnson thought.

The Post Office was already under attack from Mrs. Thatcher who wanted the London postal service investigated by the Monopolies and Mergers Commission. The management and union had to find some way to reform some of the more dubious working practices before the commission wrote its report. As a result, Improved Working Methods were introduced, which traded reductions in overtime against weekly bonuses.

Johnson convinced Slough to participate in this scheme. It seemed to him that this gave the workers a measure of control and introduced a form of what was then known as industrial democracy. While this was being discussed at the executive committee, Johnson discovered that he was the only member who knew how things actually worked in a sorting office. Consequently, Tom Jackson asked Johnson to give seminars and write a handbook, explaining IWM – though there was still considerable opposition to it throughout the ranks.

Chapter Eight – Moving On Up

Life had changed for Alan Johnson. He now wore a suit to work, just as his mother had always wanted him to. Soon he was to make his first flight on an aeroplane, when he was on his way to resolve a strike in Dundee involving the new IWM scheme.

Having mastered the details of IWM, he found it relatively easy to solve the dispute and returned south the next day with a Dundee cake and book of Robbie Burns' verse.

With the introduction of postcodes across the country, mechanization was now coming to the Post Office. But Johnson had other concerns. A kick-around with two youngsters resulted in a broken ankle, bring a premature end to his footballing career at the age of just thirty-one. This also kept him out of the office and away from resolving disputes for six weeks. However, the time off allowed him to get on with writing the IWM handbook Tom Jackson had asked him for. It was published as *The Step-by-Step Guide to IWM*. The scheme worked well enough to see off the Monopolies and Mergers Commission and, for the moment, the Post Office was safe.

Political discord was provoked locally by the Thatcher government's "right to buy" scheme. The scheme gave the Johnsons and their neighbours the right to buy their houses from the council as a discount. It was a matter of fierce debate. Alan was against it. He argued that, if they exercised their right to buy, they would be depriving future generations of the chance of having their own council house – the one thing that Lily had always dreamed of. In discussions, he generally found himself on the wrong side of the argument. Most of his neighbours bought their houses, then sold up and moved away. But the Johnsons clung onto their house and their principles.

Besides Johnson's home in Slough was handy for Heathrow airport and he became a frequent flier. He flew regularly to Northern Ireland to hold seminars and weekend courses though the Troubles were raging there. It was dangerous work as the UCW was determinedly non-sectarian and, out on the streets, postal workers were particularly vulnerable.

In 1982, Johnson drove Tom Jackson to the union meeting at Ascot where he was to announce that he was stepping down as general secretary. Other senior members of the union were also due to retire and, on the way back to London, Jackson told him that he should aim to become General Secretary. But first he would have to become a union national officer. He would have to watch his back, Jackson warned. Others had ambitions to be General Secretary and the knives were already drawn.

Johnson now had his job cut out extending the IWM scheme to parts of the country that were reluctant to embrace it. He had to travel around the nation trying to convince the recalcitrant. He also held seminars to explain the complex formulas involved, though he was a dunce at maths at school himself. Fortunately, the electronic calculator had just been introduced.

A training school was set up in a hotel the union had bought in Bournemouth. But other members of the executive committee studiously avoided it, so Johnson had the field to himself. However, his efforts won favour with the rank and file. He placated the regional managers and won the members substantial pay increases and sometimes a large lump sum covering arrears. Soon he was topping the polls in the annual executive committee elections and the ballots for the TUC and Labour Party conference delegations.

He attended the Labour Party conference for the first time in 1982. Michael Foot was leader. Johnson was an admirer, especially of his masterful two-volume biography of Aneurin Bevan, though Foot was clearly the wrong man to be leading the party into the election the following year. And that election was to be crucial. Mrs. Thatcher was already bringing in laws to curb the unions. The closed shop was to be outlawed. Strike ballots became mandatory and General Secretaries were to stand for election every five years – to be fair, a measure the postal union had already considered and rejected. Under the Thatcher government, the consensual approach to industrial relations that had operated since World War II had been thrown out of the door and the unions were under siege.

The postal union was particularly vulnerable. In 1981, telecommunications – that is, the telephone, what was left of the telegraph and other wire-based systems – had been hived off from the Post Office. Then in 1982, the government announced it was to be privatized and the field would be opened up to competition from other telecommunications companies. This went ahead after the Conservatives' landslide victory in 1983 when even Joan Lestor lost her seat. By then, Johnson was the executive of Labour's southern region, where the party came in third, behind the Conservatives and the upstart SDP-Liberal Alliance, which later became the Liberal Democrats after a poor showing in the 1987 election.

As the heads of the trade unions no longer had access to power, the members of the UCW became restive, while the officials became involved in infighting. Things became worse for the unions in the mid-1980s, when the miners' strike was soundly defeated and Rupert Murdoch broke the print unions in Fleet Street. And while the UCW opposed the privatization of British Telecom in 1984, its members bought shares.

Trade unionists were under attack from the other side too. While they wore smart suits when representing their members at Labour Party conferences, they found themselves surrounded by youths wearing denim, covered in badges supporting all manner of far-left causes. Only Arthur Scargill and the NUM executive drew applause, but it was clear that they had led their troops over a cliff.

While it was hoped that the Post Office itself was safe from the rising tide of privatization, it was divided up into four sectors – mails, counters, parcels and the Girobank. The union feared this might be the first step towards a sell-off. The only card the union was holding was that the Post Office actually made money for the Exchequer. But clearly to fend off Mrs. Thatcher, the union would have to make peace with management, so they could present a united front to the government.

Johnson was privy to the talks and watched the new general secretary Alan Tuffin, a master negotiator, in action. Sitting beside Tuffin, Johnson said that he learnt the necessity of earning the respect of the opponent, listening carefully to their arguments and using delaying tactics, such as adjournments, to think things over rather that make hasty decisions.

The upshot of the talks was an agreement called Safeguarding the Future of the Mails Business. Under it, IWM, now seen as his baby, was to be extended and Johnson got much of the credit.

Johnson's duties kept away from home a lot. He even travelled abroad to meetings of the PTTI – the Postal, Telegraph and Telephone International. Domestically, he and other members of the executive were involved in fire-fighting exercises, trying to quell the spontaneous walkouts, by then illegal, caused by the over-zealous imposition of the SFMB agreement.

In those days, wild-cat strikes were common. One was caused by the arrest of a sixty-year-old sorter after an officious Post Office manager in Preston had seen him briefly examining a holiday brochure that had been in the post. Every postal worker in the north-west walked out. Johnson was called in to sort out the situation.

In talks, the Post Office conceded that this was hardly a criminal matter. It would be handled by a disciplinary hearing where the offender would be represented by Johnson, who had already made a secret agreement that no action would result. Everyone went back to work. In such encounters, Johnson earned the trust of both the management and the workforce.

To fulfil his ambition of becoming General Secretary, he still had to become a national officer. Despite his popularity among the membership, twice he was beaten in the polls for vacant offices.

Johnson was at the Labour Party conference in Bournemouth in 1985, when leader Neil Kinnock took on Militant, saying famously: "You start with far-fetched resolutions. They are then pickled into a rigid dogma, a code, and you go through the years sticking to that, out-dated, misplaced, irrelevant to the real needs, and you end in the grotesque chaos of a Labour council – a *Labour* council! – hiring taxis to scuttle round a city handing out redundancy notices to its own workers. I'm telling you… you can't play politics with people's jobs and people's services."

This caused acrimony with the part, Even the branch in Slough had its Militant cadre. Although Johnson was a man of the left, he had little time for the firebrands on the rostrum who could not negotiation or advance the cause of the working class in any practical way.

Rather than taking political postures, the UCW tried to co-operate with the government to advance the interests of its members. It helped persuade the Post Office to accept money from the failing Youth Training Scheme to set up a Postal Cadet Scheme, guaranteeing jobs to sixteen-year-olds, though union activists, particularly those in the north, were against it. Johnson was sent to talk them round – with limited success.

When the quaintly named position of "outdoor secretary" became open, Johnson was asked to step in temporarily. And when a ballot was held, he was elected permanently to the position. Then, at last, he quit the Post Office and became an full-time employee of the union.

As his union work took up so much of his time, it was inevitable that Alan and Judy grew apart. While his life was full of travel and new challenges, she had remained at home. The children had grown up and, without him around, she had grown lonely. They talked it over and decided that it was better if they split up. After the couple divorced in 1991, Johnson married Laura Jane Patient. They had a son in 2000.

Chapter Nine – The World of Politics

Alan Johnson's career in the union continued without a hitch. In January 1992, he was elected General Secretary, the youngest in its history. Then when the government announced that it intended to privatize the Post Office, he turned the tables on them by hiring the Tories own PR guru Tim Bell – the man behind the 1979 "Labour Isn't Working" campaign – to trash the plans. As a result, the Royal Mail remained in public hands for the time being.

From his position as General Secretary, Johnson threw his net wider, becoming a director of Unity Trust Bank plc and a member of Ruskin College Oxford's governing council. He served on the General Council of the TUC and was a member of the National Executive Committee. He was also a member of the World Executive of PTTI which the UCW was affiliated to.

In 1995, he oversaw the Union of Communications Workers' merger with the National Communications Union to form the Communications Workers' Union and became its first Joint General Secretary. By then, Johnson was a political insider as a member of Labour's National Executive. Broadly seen as a Blairite, he was an advocate of modernization of the party. He was the only leader of a major union to champion the abolition of Clause Four of Labour Party Constitution that promised "the common ownership of the means of production, distribution and exchange". He even drafted a pamphlet for the Fabian Society that suggested ways the unions could loosen their links with the Labour Party.

A few months before the 1997 general election, he was approached by Tony Blair, who offered him a safe seat. Stuart Randall, the MP for West Hull and Hessle where he commanded an impregnable nine thousand majority, suddenly stood down and was subsequently elevated to the House of Lords. Johnson was parachuted in and won the seat with an increased major as Blair swept to victory.

As a back-bench MP, Johnson took an £11,000 pay cut, stepping down from his £54,000-a-year position as General Secretary of the CWU. Nevertheless, he was tipped for greater things.

"Alan is the most able union leader of his generation and Tony wanted him," said a Labour spokesman. "He will be a first class MP and a brilliant minister – he won't be a backbencher for long."

He made his maiden speech in the House of Commons about the long campaign for trawlermen's compensation, which he eventually led to success three years later. He also took up the case of the trawler *Gaul*, which sank in the North Sea in 1974 amid allegations that she was spying. This resulted in a new formal investigation in 2004.

One of Johnson's first jobs after being elected to parliament was to head the investigation into allegations that Mohammed Sarwar, the MP for Glasgow Govan, gave a bribe to another candidate in the general election campaign. Meanwhile, the Fabian pamphlet Johnson had written was dropped quietly in the bin.

He was appointed parliamentary private secretary to Dawn Primarolo, then Financial Secretary to the Treasury. It was not a marriage made in heaven. Primarolo was known as "Red Dawn" and had petitioned the Soviet government to rehabilitate Leon Trotsky. After his appointment, the *Sunday Mirror* awarded Johnson their "Worst Joke of the Year" award, when he quipped: "This is the era of a new Dawn."

He continued as her PPS when she became Paymaster General. But this position was a stepping stone. In 1999, he became a minister in the Department of Trade and Industry. From there he moved to the Department for Education and Skills as Minister for Higher Education. Many thought this was a strange appointment as he had left school at fifteen. However, he proved a cunning and persuasive campaigner in the battle to get the back benches to support "top up" university tuition fees. He argued that in forty years of free higher education the social class gap had widened rather than narrowed. Graduates should make a contribution to their degree course – £1 in every £14 spent – to help fund the expansion of higher education. He also urged the return of maintenance grants for the poorest students.

Although he did not have an O-level to his name, Johnson cut a more convincing figure among old Labour stalwarts than Charles Clarke, his hectoring, public-school-educated boss.

"I was part of the charm offensive with Charles Clarke," Johnson said. "I did the charming and he was offensive."

Before the vote, the Labour whips were so unsure of victory that Blair discussed the terms of the motion of confidence that would have followed such a major defeat.

Thanks to Johnson, the measure was carried, but by just five votes. Blair rewarded him with a Cabinet post as Secretary of State for Work and Pensions, making him the first ex-union General Secretary to join the Cabinet since Frank Cousins in 1964.

It was not an easy position to step into. The Child Support Agency was in virtual meltdown and there was a £50 billion shortfall in the nation's pensions provision – some twelve million people were not saving enough for their retirement. But when the subject was debated in the House of Commons, Johnson crushed the Tories' spokesman David Willetts, citing Labour's achievement of lifting two million pensioners out of abject poverty. Meanwhile he showed a killer instinct when he threw the Child Support Agency boss, Doug Smith, to the wolves on live television in front of a House of Common's select committee.

Following that performance, there was talk of his possible leadership candidacy when Tony Blair stood down. It was said that he was being groomed for the top job by the "Anyone But Brown" caucus.

"Don't put money on it," he told the press. "It's science fiction – but nice science fiction. I got rid of my leadership tendencies in the Communication Workers Union. I've got it out of my system. I wanted to get to the top there. I don't really want to get to the top here. It's just fantasy."

The job he really wanted, he said, was to be manager of Queen's Park Rangers. At the time, it was noted, he was reading Roy Jenkins' biography of Churchill, perhaps picking up a few tips on late-developing political careers.

After the Labour Party won a third term in 2005, Johnson became Secretary of State for Trade and Industry – he was to have been Productivity, Energy and Industry Secretary until someone realized that the acronym would have spelt out "PENIS".

In the reshuffle the following year, he became Secretary of State for Education and Skills. In this role, he urged parents to play a bigger role in their child's education with his "Every Parent Matters" strategy. He said parenting had been a "no go" area for government, but people needed help. Research had shown that three-quarters of parents wanted advice on bringing up their children.

From his own experience, Johnson believed that one of the most important things a parent could do to boost their children's chances in life was to read to them. This was a simple solution, he said, "but in a busy world it doesn't happen enough. Thirty per cent of parents don't read regularly with their children – a vital but missed opportunity to boost their children's development. We watch an average of four hours television a day. If we read to children for just a tenth of this every day, we'd give their chances a massive boost."

He gave his backing to the National Year of Reading the following year, hoping it would bring about a step change in attitudes to reading for advancement and pleasure.

"Reading opens up a world of opportunities and books are the foundation on which we can build other learning," he said. "Reading should be a source of pleasure in itself, as well as an essential support for increasing the life chances of children."

This certainly echoed his own life experience.

Extra advice and support was to be offered to parents with numeracy and literacy problems, encouraging them to participate in learning activities with their children. A particular effort was made to get working parents, especially fathers, to be more involved with their children. Schemes highlighted by Johnson include one where fathers worked with their children on allotments, visited sports facilities together or took part in music projects. However, the parenting strategy, he said, had to be "bias-free", adding: "It's what parents do, not who they are, that makes the difference."

Johnson had already opened up a debate about the role of the family after the then leader of the opposition David Cameron suggested fathers should be forced to support their children and Prime Minister Tony Blair called for "intervention" at an early age to tackle problem children. While refusing to stigmatize "alternative lifestyles" or single parents, there has been an underlying agreement between the political parties that the traditional family structure of a married mother and father raising children was the best option. Johnson challenged this assumption head on, suggesting that other family models could be equally effective and that there was nothing essentially superior about the traditional unit.

"While marriage represents the pinnacle of a strong relationship," he said, "that does not mean that all children from married couples fare well, nor that every other kind of alternate family structure is irretrievably doomed to fail."

He argued that the debate centring around marriage was looking at the issue through the wrong end of the telescope.

"It's the child that is at the centre of this, it's the parenting that matters, it's not the form of the relationship," he said.

He particularly attacked Cameron's suggestion that tax breaks to encourage marriage were the way forward.

"It's wrong to suggest that tax and legislation makes relationships, it's not, it's love," he said.

He also branded the old married couples' allowance, abolished by Labour, as "pernicious and judgmental" because it discriminated against the third of all children whose parents are not married.

Nevertheless, he was at odds with Tony Blair, who continued to urge that "marriage is good". This was seen as the opening in Johnson's bid to become deputy leader when John Prescott stepped down.

Johnson also warned of the dangers of the new system of diplomas that the government were introducing, telling the Association of School and College Leaders conference: "Things could go horribly wrong, particularly as we are keeping A-levels and GCSEs. The decision was taken in the interests of diversity, so young people have choice. That does mean there is a danger of the diplomas becoming, if you like, the secondary modern compared to the grammar."

317

This drew fire from the chair of the Commons education select committee, Labour MP Barry Sheerman.

"I don't think it is for the secretary of state to spread alarm and despondency," he said. "I would prefer the secretary of state to lead from the front and accentuate the positives – get off his backside and do something about it."

But the general secretary of the ASCL called Johnson's comments "refreshingly honest".

He got teachers on side by recommending a new pay structure for part-time teachers, giving them the same contractual conditions as their full-time colleagues. This meant that part-time teachers in England and Wales would be paid for work they did outside the class, such as preparing lessons and marking.

After standing aside in the race to become leader of the party, saying he was backing the favourite Gordon Brown, Johnson stood in the contest for deputy leader.

"It is, of course, a matter for the party to decide who the leader's going to be, but my view is Gordon is a towering political figure," he said. "It's not a position that I ever sought and there is a superb candidate in Gordon Brown."

As a deputy leader, he said, he hoped to "complement, help, cajole and assist" the party leader and occasionally tell them what they do not want to hear. "I think that's an important role and that's one I want to put myself forward for."

318

Johnson received the most nominations for the post and led the ballot in the first four rounds of voting. But in the fifth he was pipped at the post by Harriet Harman, who won by just 0.8 per cent.

Self-effacing as ever, Johnson said he was not disappointed for himself, but was disappointed for his campaign team. Ms. Harman would be a "very good deputy leader," he said. "I think there was a big view in the party that it needed to be a woman."

When Gordon Brown took over as Prime Minister in June 2007 he made Johnson Secretary of State for Health. The following year, he found himself embroiled in the controversy over breast-cancer-sufferer Debbie Hirst who was warned that she would be denied treatment on the NHS if she sold her house to buy the expensive anti-cancer drug Avastin. Johnson supported the NHS position, saying that patients "cannot, in one episode of treatment, be treated on the NHS and then allowed, as part of the same episode and the same treatment, to pay money for more drugs". It was, he said, against "a founding principle of the NHS... that someone is either a private patient or an NHS patient".

He also ran into difficulties when Maidstone & Tunbridge Wells NHS Trust agreed to pay £250,000 compensation to their chief executive after sacking her over an outbreak of C.difficile in their hospitals. Johnson intervened, blocking the payment. However, the payment went ahead after the case reached the court of appeal.

In June 2009, he was appointed Home Secretary. Now he could return to Dorneywood, this time as a resident. But almost immediately he was involved in controversy when he sacked

Professor David Nutt as chairman of the Advisory Council of the Misuse of Drugs.

Professor Nutt had claimed that ecstasy, LSD and cannabis were less dangerous than alcohol and tobacco.

"Alcohol ranks as the fifth most harmful drug after heroin, cocaine, barbiturates and methadone. Tobacco is ranked ninth," he wrote in the paper from the centre for crime and justice studies at King's College, London. "Cannabis, LSD and ecstasy, while harmful, are ranked lower at eleventh, fourteenth and eighteenth respectively."

He complained that politicians were distorting and devaluing evidence supplied by research into illicit drugs after the previous Home Secretary, Jaqui Smith, had reclassified cannabis from Class C to Class B, ignoring the recommendations of his committee, and rejecting the scientific advice to downgrade MDMA from Class A.

Alan Johnson wrote to Professor Nutt, saying: "It is important that the government's messages on drugs are clear and as an advisor you do nothing to undermine public understanding of them. As my lead advisor on drug harms I am afraid the manner in which you have acted runs contrary to your responsibilities. I cannot have public confusion between scientific advice and policy and have therefore lost confidence in your ability to advise me as Chair of the ACMD. I would therefore ask you to step down with immediate effect."

Johnson's position worsened over the next few months as another seven members of the ACMD quit, complaining that decisions on the classification of drug mephedrone were made due to media and political pressure.

"There's not been proper consideration given to the broader justice and political aspects of making a drug Class B and criminalizing maybe tens of thousands of young people," Johnson said. "I'm not surprised that people think it's all been done for political reasons rather than scientific or health reasons."

Shadow Home Secretary Chris Grayling said the relationship between the government and the ACMD had become "utterly shambolic", but reserved faint praise for Johnson.

"After all the chaos of the last few months, it finally looked as if Alan Johnson might be getting things back into shape again," he said. "The decision on mephedrone was the right one, but this latest resignation suggests pretty clearly that the Home Secretary has been completely unable to restore his relationship with the experts who advise him."

When British resident and former Guantanamo Bay detainee Binyam Mohamed claimed that MI5 officers had fed questions to his CIA torturers in Pakistan and Morocco, Johnson warned that any police investigation into the matter could jeopardize Britain's national security. He said the claims were "baseless, groundless accusations". The courts did not agree. Binyam Mohamed was given £1 million in compensation by the government, rather than investigating the matter further.

Despite these political difficulties, key members of the Cabinet suspected Johnson of plotting to unseat Gordon Brown.

"However, he steadfastly denied he was interested in the top job, and on more than one occasion stated he did not feel he was up to it," said the *Sunday Telegraph*. "Despite this lack of ambition, several Labour MPs thought his easy going manner would make him a more popular leader than Mr Brown, particularly in marginal seats in the south of England, and would give the party a better chance of retaining power in this year's election. Several urged him to oppose Mr Brown."

Nevertheless, he remained loyal into the 2010 election and beyond.

Chapter Ten – Into the Wilderness

In May 2010 the Labour government was swept from office, but Johnson stayed on the front bench as Shadow Home Secretary. Despite this electoral setback, he still appeared to be the coming man in the Labour Party. Within a week, the *London Evening Standard* were tipping Alan Johnson to be a candidate to take on Boris Johnson in the election to be Mayor of London which was still two years away. It would be "Johnson versus Johnson," the paper said.

Alan Johnson was well qualified for the job. A Londoner born and bred, he was a "big-hitter" from the Blair-Brown Cabinet. And he was certainly available. He had already backed out of the forthcoming leadership race, saying it was time for the "next generation" of politicians to take up the fight against the Conservatives nationally and backing David Miliband for the post.

According to the *Standard*: "Allies of the former Home Secretary would love to see a 'Johnson v Johnson' contest and believe their man is the type of big figure needed to knock out Boris. A skilled media performer, AJ's easy charm and quick wit would ensure a mouth-watering clash with Bojo. But he also has impeccable Londoner credentials.

"Born and bred in Notting Hill when it was an impoverished collection of tenements rather than the Cameroonian haven it is today, he was brought up by his teenage sister after his mother died.

He then became a London postie – and can still remember the streets he pounded across the city – before rising to become leader of the postal workers' union and then an MP."

He did not take the bait and backed Oona King instead. After Ken Livingston won the nomination, there was speculation that the new Labour leader Ed Miliband might deselect Livingston and put Johnson in his place. Livingston was sceptical.

"Alan Johnson is a lovely fellow," he said, "but to do this you have to be absolutely ruthless, relentless, and driven. No one ever accused Alan of that."

Johnson later revealed that he had never considered running for Mayor of London. He was the MP for Hull and that was where his allegiance lay. Nor would he run for mayor in 2016 as he wanted to stay on as an MP.

By then, he had withdrawn from frontline politics. After Labour's defeat in 2010, he threw himself behind the campaign for electoral reform. He wrote an article for the *Observer* condemning Nick Clegg for going into the coalition without insisting on some form of proportional representation.

The following month, the *Sunday Telegraph* were saying that Labour's "lost leader" was considering standing down from his Westminster seat and fighting a by-election on the issue of proportional representation.

"Mr. Johnson, who was the favoured candidate of many Labour MPs to replace Gordon Brown as prime minister, has always been a passionate advocate of electoral reform," the paper said.

In the run-up to the Labour leadership contest, he told the *Hull Daily Mail*: "I may not put myself forward for the shadow cabinet elections and am thinking about going on to the back benches. I might be able to do something from the sidelines on the proportional representation issue. I think this is a real time of progress on that."

Fellow Labour MPs thought any attempt to force a by-election was risky. In 2008, Conservative Shadow Home Secretary David Davis had resigned and forced a by-elector on the issue of the erosion of civil liberties.

"It's hard to see that Alan would do something like that," said one Labour MP. "It sounds barking. David Davis did it and put a giant dent in his career. Having said that, Alan is absolutely a hundred per cent committed to voting reform and I suppose he might just be tempted into a grand gesture."

He didn't. But he did support the "Yes to fairer votes" campaign in the run-up to the referendum on 5 May 2011, appearing on the platform of the headline London event alongside Ed Miliband.

Despite being the first MP to back David Miliband in the leadership election, in October 2010, Johnson was invited by Ed Miliband to join his first Shadow Cabinet as Shadow Chancellor, over Ed Balls and his wife Yvette Cooper. Both Balls, who had been a leadership contender, and Cooper, who had topped the Shadow Cabinet poll, had been tipped for the job.

Johnson quickly demonstrated that he was a Miliband loyalist.

"Since his election as leader, Ed has demonstrated real strength of character and determination to unify and lead," he told the press.

"We are both passionate about a new kind of politics where we will not disagree with our political opponents for the sake of it. These are testing times and we will be a responsible opposition acting in the national interest... Ed and I will work together to build a plan for growth and for jobs in our economy. We will offer a real and responsible alternative to the dangerous plans of this coalition government, which is damaging the economic future of millions of families."

In his first major speech in the post, he advocated an extra levy on bankers of £3.5 billion. Conservative proposal, he said, "meant families take the strain while bankers grab the bonuses. There's no justification for such an unfair sharing of the burden."

However, Johnson was clearly ill-suited to the job. The BBC reported that "his economic credentials had been brought into question after several recent gaffes. In an interview he appeared not to know the rate of National Insurance paid by employers, and he was also reported to have clashed with his party leader over the policy of introducing a graduate tax to replace university tuition fees."

After less than four months in the job, Johnson stood down, citing personal reasons. He had discovered that his wife had been having an affair with his police bodyguard while he had been Home Secretary.

Johnson issued a statement saying: "I have found it difficult to cope with personal issues in my private life while carrying out an important front bench role."

He told the *Hull Daily Mail* that sorting out problems in his personal life was more important than fighting the Government over the economy.

"I don't think that I could have coped properly," he said. "You know you have to do your job properly. If you are trying to deal with your job as an MP, deal with your job as a frontbench spokesman in the shadow cabinet and shadow chancellor and at the same time you have got lots of problems to sort out at home, you can't do all three. You have to think about that and I thought, I am going to stay being a member of parliament. I need to sort our personal problems, so the shadow chancellor's position had to go."

Labour leader Ed Miliband told the BBC he had accepted his resignation "with great regret" and deputy leader Harriet Harman told BBC Radio 4's Today programme that Johnson's departure was "a very sad loss to our front bench in the Labour Party but I also think he's a loss to frontline British politics. He was universally liked and admired and we will very much miss him."

Even David Cameron was sympathetic.

"Obviously, I am very sorry for Alan because he has given a huge amount of service in public life, on the frontline," he said. "He's one of the more cheerful and optimistic characters in politics. I am sure he will go on doing a good job for his constituents and being an MP, and I hope he is able to sort out all the things he wants to. We will miss him on the front bench."

The *Independent* pointed out that, while it was relatively common for politicians to be forced out of office because they have been

327

caught cheating on their wives, Johnson was the first to resign because of a looming sex scandal in which he was the aggrieved party.

Johnson later admitted that he did not like the job of Shadow Chancellor and was surprised when Ed Miliband had offered it to him.

"I was glad to get out," he said. "I took it because I thought, 'What an extraordinary gesture, that he wants me there'. But my heart wasn't in it. I didn't like the job."

He was replaced by Gordon Brown's former Treasury advisor Ed Balls.

Johnson's protection officer PC Paul Rice was suspended from duty and later dismissed from police service following an internal investigation and a misconduct hearing. Johnson defended his "poor wife" who he said was upset by all the attention created by the scandal. She was granted a divorce in 2014, after two years separation.

Johnson had moved on, starting a new relationship with fifty-year-old award-winning businesswoman who was the boss of translation agency Language is Everything in Hull. He revealed the relationship in a local newspaper interview celebrating award of the MBE for services to business and the Humber area.

After Johnson's divorce Ed Miliband approached him and asked him if he was interested in returning to front-line politics. Johnson said no.

"What about freelancing?" asked Miliband.

"I am happy to go round the country, campaigning, talking to parties," he said, though he was frustrated that Labour had not been more effective in attacking Chancellor George Osbourne over the economy. Miliband, he said, should make "a couple of big speeches… just taking the whole thing apart".

By then, Johnson had embarked on a literary career. The first volume of his autobiography, *The Boy: A Memoir of Childhood*, published in 2013, won the Royal Society of Literature's Ondaadtje Prize for a literary work "evoking the spirit of a place" and the Orwell prize for political writing, beating Charles Moore's account of Mrs. Thatcher's early life.

In a review in the *Guardian*, former MP Chris Mullin said the book was "the biography of a politician like no other… from time to time, one has to pinch oneself to recall that this is not an account of childhood in Victorian England, but of life in the England of the 1950s and 60s. Far from being a misery memoir, it is beautifully observed, humorous, moving, uplifting; told with a dry, self-deprecating wit and not a trace of self-pity."

Accepting the prize, Johnson said that he had set out to "recapture north Kensington from Notting Hill", noting that "Julia Roberts and Hugh Grant were not often seen down our way… People lived sixteen in a house, but you were forced into a community, and were looking after people who couldn't look after themselves."

The second volume of his autobiography, *Please, Mr Postman*, was published in 2014. The *Independent* said that the book was "a wonderful elegy for a life that has only just passed into history. A time when nobody drank at home, when Post Office vans required double de-clutching and when the 'fax machine – believe it or not – was seen as a serious threat to our future'."

In it, he looks back at a time when the strike-happy officials in his own union were "like pilots who knew how to take off but who'd never been taught to land". He also points out that Arthur Scargill may have been right about the Coal Board's plan to close pits. But, he says: "The job of a trade-union leader isn't to predict rain, it's to build a bloody ark."

In it he gives a clue to why his advancement up the political ladder was so slow and why he did not have the ruthlessness to seize the top job when it was within his grasp.

"My personality was steeped in the self-effacement that held back so many working-class people," he said.

But then, Alan Johnson has read Roy Jenkins' biography of Winston Churchill and knows that Churchill did not become Prime Minster for the first time until he was sixty-five. He still claimed to be bereft of ambition. Being Prime Minister is a "godawful job," Johnson said. Nor was he planning to revive his musical career, saying that he had not touched a guitar for the ten years he had been in Cabinet.

What drove Alan Johnson was never a hunger for power. The final tribute should come from his sister, Linda, who said he inherited his decency and determination to fight for others from their mother.

"I remember remarking on the sense of justice and fairness he'd inherited from Mum," she said. "Even though we could have gone off the rails when Mum died, we were doing exactly what she would have wanted – making a difference to the people around us. She would be extremely proud of him for getting where he is today."

28801777R00188

Printed in Great Britain
by Amazon